The Wailing Lighthouse Game

based on Enid Blyton's
Five go to Demon's Rocks

Illustrated by Gary Rees

HODDER AND STOUGHTON
LONDON SYDNEY AUCKLAND TORONTO

British Library Cataloguing in Publication Data

The wailing lighthouse game.—(Adventure games book)
   1. Adventure games—Juvenile literature
   I. Rees, Gary   II. Blyton, Enid. Five go to Demon's Rocks
   III. Series
   793.9   GV1203

   ISBN 0-340-39653-9

First published 1986
Second impression 1988

Published by Hodder and Stoughton Children's Books,
a division of Hodder and Stoughton Ltd,
Mill Road, Dunton Green, Sevenoaks, Kent TN13 2YJ

Photoset by Rowland Phototypesetting Ltd,
Bury St Edmunds, Suffolk

Printed in Great Britain by Hazell, Watson & Viney Ltd.
Member of BPCC plc,
Aylesbury, Bucks

You have often read about the Famous Five's adventures . . . now here's your chance to take part in one!

This time YOU are in charge. YOU have to work out the clues, read the maps, crack the codes. Whether The Five solve the mystery or not is in your hands.

You will not necessarily solve the mystery on your first attempt. It may well take several goes. Keep trying, though, and you will eventually be successful.

Even when you *have* solved the mystery, the game can still be played again. For there are many different routes to the solution – and each route involves different clues and adventures.

So the game can be played over and over. As many times as you like!

HOW TO PLAY

To solve the mystery, you have to go with The Five on an adventure through the book. You do this by starting at PARAGRAPH ONE and then following the instructions to other paragraphs.

Many of the paragraphs will ask you to work out some sort of clue. You do not have to work out every one of the clues to solve the final mystery . . . but the more you manage, the more you're likely to be successful. The fewer clues you crack, the less chance of completing the adventure.

To help you work out the clues, there are several pieces of equipment available – a torch, a measuring tape, a map and a codebook. You can start with only *one* of these EQUIPMENT CARDS but you will often pick up others as the game goes along. Occasionally, however, you will be asked to give some up as well.

To hold your EQUIPMENT CARDS during the adventure, there is a RUCKSACK CARD. This will tell you exactly which EQUIPMENT CARDS you have for use at any one time (so, after they've helped in solving a particular clue, always remember to return them to your rucksack!). Any EQUIPMENT CARDS not in your rucksack **cannot be used or consulted** – and therefore should be kept out of play.

Of course, no Famous Five adventure could take place without provisions. You are therefore given three PICNIC CARDS. These are to be kept in the slit of the LUNCHBOX CARD.

Every time The Five eat or lose some of their provisions during the adventure, you must remove one of your PICNIC CARDS from the LUNCHBOX CARD. When there are no PICNIC CARDS left in your LUNCHBOX, the provisions have run out and so you cannot possibly continue with the adventure. The game is over and you will have to start again from the beginning.

READY TO START

The Famous Five are JULIAN (the biggest and eldest), DICK, GEORGE (real name Georgina, but she always wanted to be a boy), ANNE and George's dog, TIMMY.

They are spending part of their summer holidays at George's place – Kirrin Cottage, situated in a beautiful bay on the Cornish coast. George's father, who is a scientist, isn't too pleased at this, however. He and a friend of his, Professor Hayling, want to use the cottage to conduct some important scientific experiments and they are finding the presence of the children a bit of a distraction. Hoping to be rid of them for a day, the Professor therefore tells them about Wailing Lighthouse, several miles further up the coast.

According to legend, the caves near this disused lighthouse are the hiding place for a wealth of treasure. The treasure was originally looted from wrecked ships which were deliberately forced on to the rocks by a gang of evil men. They did this by overpowering the lighthouse keeper and dousing the lamp so that the ships wouldn't know there was any danger there. This is why it is called *Wailing* Lighthouse – wailing for the poor sailors who lost their lives. And, often, the wind swirling round the lighthouse seems to make just such a sound!

The professor tells them that there might not be anything in the legend, of course . . . but he knows that he has said enough to get The Five hooked! Rumours of hidden treasure? How could they possibly resist!

So, they immediately prepare to make an expedition to Wailing Lighthouse . . .

To join them on this expedition, you will first of all need to put on your rucksack. So pick out the RUCKSACK CARD and keep it near you. You must now choose a piece of equipment to take with you. The Five each have a map, a torch, a measuring tape and a codebook – but you can start with only *one* of these. Which do you think would be the most useful? Insert the EQUIPMENT CARD you have chosen into the slit of your RUCKSACK CARD and keep the remaining three EQUIPMENT CARDS out of play until told you can pick them up.

Now for the provisions. George's mother kindly prepares for The Five a delicious picnic of sandwiches, cherry cake and ginger beer. Put the three PICNIC CARDS into the slit of your LUNCHBOX CARD. Don't forget to remove a picnic card every time The Five eat or lose some of their provisions.

Remember: When there are no PICNIC CARDS left in your LUNCHBOX, the adventure has to stop and you must start the game all over again.

Good Luck!

'Do you think there really *is* treasure hidden somewhere in the caves?' Dick asked his brother excitedly as they all set out from Kirrin Cottage. 'Or do you think it's just an old yarn passed down from generation to generation?' Julian said it *could* be true – the Cornish coast was certainly famous for its number of deliberate shipwrecks. This made them feel even more hopeful but of course they had to *find* the lighthouse and caves first – and they suddenly realised that Professor Hayling hadn't told them how to get there! 'Anyone got any ideas?' George asked. As it turned out, they *all* had ideas – George too, and even Timmy by the look of him! – and so they had a quick discussion to decide whose idea sounded best.

Throw the special FAMOUS FIVE DICE to decide whose idea they should follow – then turn to the appropriate number. If you throw 'Mystery', you must turn to that number instead.

JULIAN thrown	go to 268
DICK thrown	go to 69
GEORGE thrown	go to 148
ANNE thrown	go to 36
TIMMY thrown	go to 227
MYSTERY thrown	go to 163

The footpath they were on hugged the line of the cliffs for another half mile or so before it suddenly divided, one branch shooting off inland. 'We obviously want to keep to the branch that sticks to the cliff-tops,' said Julian, but Dick wasn't so sure. He said that maybe the path that went inland provided a *short cut* to the lighthouse. 'It might mean missing out a lot of unnecessary coves and headlands,' he remarked. They were still trying to decide which branch to follow when Anne noticed a message chiselled into a flat rock in the ground! It was in code, though, and so it needed their codebooks to work out what it said.

Do you have a CODEBOOK in your RUCKSACK? If so, use it to find out what the message on the rock said by decoding the instruction below. If you don't have one, go to 72 instead.

The 160 paces brought The Five into the middle of a sand-bunker! 'This thing that can help must be underneath the sand somewhere,' Dick commented, beginning to kick it up with his shoe. The others all did the same, *Anne* finally being the one to uncover something. 'Look, it's a torch,' she exclaimed rather disappointedly as she showed it to the others. '*That's* what the message meant about it being a help in the search for the treasure!' Julian said it wasn't that disappointing, though, because the torch was a lot more powerful than any of theirs, and he suggested they take it with them.

If you don't already have it, put the TORCH CARD into your RUCKSACK. Now go to 191.

If you don't already have it, put the TORCH CARD into your RUCKSACK. Now go to 191.

4

They were still trying to find their torches in their rucksacks, however, when the soldier suddenly disappeared again. Since he hadn't seen them frantically waving their hands or anything, he obviously must have assumed they were all right . . . which of course they were. Well, except for feeling a little hungry again! But Anne soon saw to that by suggesting they stop for a quick sandwich. The others all thought it a very good idea!

Take a PICNIC CARD from your LUNCHBOX. Now go to 90.

Take a PICNIC CARD from your LUNCHBOX. Now go to 90.

Plucking up his courage, *Dick* said he would enter the cave first and he led the way into the gaping entrance. As it quickly grew darker, however, he began to wish he hadn't been so rash! He turned round to the others. 'Er – before we go any further,' he said, searching for an excuse to delay it a bit, 'perhaps we ought to look up the caves on our maps while there's still enough light to read them. It would be interesting to find out exactly where they are!'

Use your MAP to find out which square the caves are in – then follow the instruction. If you don't have one in your RUCK-SACK, you'll have to guess which instruction to follow.

If you think E2	go to 284
If you think E1	go to 250
If you think D1	go to 153

As Dick shrugged off his rucksack to look for his map, he suddenly did exactly what George had warned against; he lost his footing on the slippery cave floor! The others heard an ominous rattling sound from his lunchbox as they helped him up again. 'I've got a horrible feeling your ginger beer bottle's broken,' Julian told him. He was absolutely right. When Dick held his lunchbox up, a foamy liquid dripped from the corner!

Take a PICNIC CARD from your LUNCHBOX. Now go to 27.

As soon as they had found the cliff steps, they started to climb down. The steps were very steep and Julian told them to tread very slowly and carefully. About a third of the way from the bottom, however, Dick's foot suddenly slipped and he only managed to regain his balance by letting go of his lunchbox. It rolled all the way to the cliff bottom! As soon as they had reached the bottom themselves, Dick ran over to it to check on the damage. The lunchbox itself hardly had a scratch but the bottle of ginger beer inside was smashed to smithereens!

Take a PICNIC CARD from your LUNCHBOX. Now go to 275. (Remember: when there are no picnic cards left in your lunchbox, the game is over and you must start again.)

'Look, the lighthouse is only round the next corner!' Dick said excitedly when he was the first to find the sea-arch on his map. 'We should be able to see it very soon!' So, as soon as they had put their maps away again, they hurried along the cliff edge. Suddenly, there was the lighthouse – standing grey, silent, and eerie on its little rocky island just out to sea! *Go to 25.*

They finally decoded the message as: *THERE SHOULD BE ENOUGH TREASURE TO MAKE US ALL RICH FOR THE REST OF OUR LIVES. BUT WE MUST KEEP QUIET ABOUT IT OR WE'LL HAVE TO HAND IT IN TO SOME ROTTEN MUSEUM!* The children all looked rather concerned at this. It sounded as if a gang of villains was on the hunt for the treasure as well! 'And the fact that the message is in Jeremiah's boat,' Dick added excitedly, 'suggests that *he* is one of those villains!' Julian was a little more cautious in jumping to this conclusion, however, saying the gang might have used his boat to pass messages without his knowledge. But, when George later found a measuring tape hidden in the bottom of the boat, their suspicions about Jeremiah increased again. Could this be to help him in the search for the treasure?

If you don't already have it, put the MEASURE CARD into your RUCKSACK. Now go to 185.

10

The Five waved goodbye to Jeremiah as they pushed his rowing-boat into the sea. With the two boys taking it in turns at the oars, heaving against the waves, they at last reached the little rocky island. 'Gosh, the lighthouse looks even eerier close to!' George remarked as they all stepped ashore and stared up at its silent mass. They climbed a few rocky steps to its base, finding a door there. After pushing it open, they nervously discussed who was going to walk through first!

Throw THE FAMOUS FIVE DICE to decide which one it's to be.

JULIAN thrown	go to 156
DICK thrown	go to 282
GEORGE thrown	go to 193
ANNE thrown	go to 234
TIMMY thrown	go to 93
MYSTERY thrown	go to 127

11

'Only another couple of metres to go,' Dick called from the front as they measured the forty metres up the steps. 'Everyone keep their eyes open!' He studied each of the next few steps very carefully before treading on it, suddenly spotting a length of fine trip-wire. 'What a good job we had our measuring tapes!' he exclaimed as he cut it through with his penknife. 'I wouldn't be surprised if this has been put here by someone else who has heard about the treasure being in the lighthouse – someone who wants to make sure others don't come looking for it!' *Go to 94.*

Continuing to climb the spiral steps, The Five passed through and explored several small rooms – one above the other – until they finally reached in the lamp-room at the very top. This one was far brighter, the sun pouring in through the glass surround! Running outside the glass was a small balcony and they wondered if there was any way on to it. 'Yes, here we are!' called George. 'This pane of glass has got a handle and hinges to it, as if it opens like a sort of door!' *Go to 302.*

They had measured less than half the distance instructed by the message when they found that they were back where they started from, having walked the complete way round the wall! 'Oh, it must have been someone's stupid joke!' said George crossly, and she was so annoyed that she rubbed the message off. And it was only when she'd had a long drink of her ginger beer that she was prepared to join the others in continuing the search of the room!

Take a PICNIC CARD from your LUNCHBOX. Now go to 62.

14

As Julian reached down into Dick's rucksack, however, his other hand nearly slipped from the rung! He just managed to grip it properly again but, in doing so, he accidentally kicked Dick's head. Dick gave such a start that he made his map fall from his open rucksack. As they watched it disappear into the blackness below, the two boys decided they had better try and go down the shaft without a torch. There were likely to be further accidents otherwise!

If you have it, remove the MAP from your RUCKSACK. Now go to 31.

15

'This must be it!' said Anne, finding a stone bridge on her map and showing it to the others. Julian now had a think for a moment, wondering what to do. 'We've got to try and find a way out so we can inform the police about this gang before their plane arrives,' he told them. 'Since we're never going to be able to move all these boulders, I think our best chance is to return to the lighthouse and have another go at that locked door!' Just as they were about to start their run back along the tunnel, Timmy spotted an old measuring tape hidden amongst the boulders!

If you don't already have it, put the MEASURE CARD into your RUCKSACK. Now go to 196.

16

Their maps showed that the campsite was only about half a mile from Kirrin Bay and it wasn't long before they reached it. They immediately went up to one of the campers, asking if he knew a short cut to Wailing Lighthouse. 'Yes, I think you take that footpath over there,' he replied, scratching his head. 'The one that passes behind that clump of trees.' To thank him for his help, Dick offered the camper one of his sandwiches. 'That's very kind of you,' the man told him as he gratefully accepted. 'My favourite, too – ham and tomato!

Take a PICNIC CARD from your LUNCHBOX. Now go to 53.

17

'Those voices are coming from one of the caves in the cliff!' Julian began to tell the others excitedly. 'This undersea tunnel must come out there – or, at least, used to before it was sealed off with these boulders. It was probably built originally to provide an alternative route into the lighthouse, for when the sea was too rough to cross. Anyway – the treasure *is* in the caves after all and those men we can hear must be intending to loot it!' The others were convinced Julian was right, saying that it was a pity they couldn't get past the boulders to surprise the men in the act. Since they couldn't, though, they decided to return immediately to the lighthouse and try and think of some other way of getting out – so they could inform the police! *Go to 160.*

Timmy suddenly started to bark excitedly, pointing his paw into the darkness. 'What is it, Timmy?' George asked. 'Have you spotted the cliff-tops? Yes, you have! Look – everybody!' The police boat immediately came ashore and they all leapt out on to the pebbles. They were halfway to the foot of the steps when they noticed a sheet stretched out across the beach, anchored down by rocks. There was a huge coded message painted across it! 'I bet that was put there by the gang,' said Julian excitedly, and he slipped off his rucksack so he could take out his codebook.

Use your CODEBOOK CARD to find out what the message said by decoding the instruction below. If you don't have a CODEBOOK in your RUCKSACK, go to 258 instead.

19

While they were looking for their maps, the moon came out from behind a cloud and made something to their right glisten. 'I know what that is,' the sergeant exclaimed. 'It's the river! You won't be needing your maps after all, children. The stone bridge obviously *crosses* the river and so all we have to do is follow it!' They were very soon approaching the bridge, just able to make out several shadowy figures standing on it. 'They must be the gang!' the sergeant whispered tensely as he quickly made them all hide behind a boulder. 'We'll wait here until their plane arrives!' While they were waiting, George noticed that she didn't have her lunchbox with her. She must have left it back at the cliff-tops!

Take a PICNIC CARD from your LUNCHBOX. Now go to 134. (Remember: when there are no picnic cards left in your lunchbox the game is over, and you must start again.)

20

The children carefully packed their maps away again, ready to continue. They hadn't walked much further, however, when Anne suggested they stop for a drink of their ginger beer. 'I know we really ought to save it for later,' she said, 'but my lunchbox is feeling quite heavy!' The others said that their lunchboxes felt quite heavy too and therefore agreed to Anne's suggestion.

Take a PICNIC CARD from your LUNCHBOX. Now go to 199.

Julian volunteered to run over to the bird-watcher, telling the others he would be as quick as he could. When he reached him, however, the bird-watcher said he had never heard of Wailing Lighthouse. 'Hang on a minute,' he added suddenly, just as Julian was about to make his way back again. 'You see that large rock over there, there's something about "Wailing Lighthouse" chiselled into the surface. The trouble is, the rest of the writing seems to be in some sort of code!'

Do you have a CODEBOOK in your RUCKSACK? If so, use it to find out what the writing on the rock said by decoding the instruction below. If you don't have one, go to 260 instead.

Locating the harbour on their maps, the children saw that they still hadn't come very far yet. 'I thought we'd be a good third of the way there by now,' moaned George. 'Instead, we're only about an eighth!' She then put forward the idea of making their way down to the harbour and seeing if they could hire a boat to take them round to the lighthouse. 'No, that would take even longer,' Julian said, disappointing her. 'Besides, the sea's looking a bit rough at the moment and it might be dangerous.' *Go to 2.*

23

The coded message *was* about the way to Wailing Lighthouse! They worked it out as: *FOR WAILING LIGHTHOUSE, CONTINUE TOWARD THE PILE OF ROCKS IN THE DISTANCE.* 'That must be them,' George said excitedly, pointing to half a dozen large boulders on the next ridge. As they were trekking towards the boulders, Dick noticed that Julian was looking rather perturbed. 'It's that message,' Julian explained when Dick asked him the cause. 'It looks very much like someone else is interested in Wailing Lighthouse!' *Go to 39.*

24

George gave a sudden click of her fingers. 'I know what those bangs are!' she exclaimed. 'I was right – it *is* shooting. But it's nothing to be worried about because it's from an army rifle range!' As if to prove her right, at that very moment a soldier appeared on the ridge. Suddenly noticing them all standing there in the middle of nowhere, he shouted to them, asking if they were lost or needed help. They tried to shout back that everything was all right but their voices weren't as strong as his. 'I know,' said Dick with a sudden burst of inspiration, 'we'll use our torches to tell him in Morse code!'

Use your TORCH CARD to flash this message to the soldier by placing exactly over the shape below – then follow the instruction. If you don't have a TORCH in your RUCKSACK, go to 4 instead.

25

They were so excited by their discovery of the lighthouse that for a while they forgot why they had *really* come all this way. It wasn't for the lighthouse but the caves nearby! Suddenly George remembered this and she scanned the cliffs far below them, her eye stopping at two huge chasms. 'Look, they must be the caves!' she exclaimed with delight. 'Can you see? At the end of that long narrow bay down there!' *Go to 275.*

As hard as they studied their maps, though, there was no sign of any youth hostel! 'Surely they would mark something like that,' Dick said, scratching his head. Then Julian suddenly realised. 'Of course!' he told them. 'If the youth hostel is no longer in use, then they probably don't bother to show it on newer maps like ours. It would just mislead people.' So they put their maps away again but, before they continued on their way, Anne suggested they have a little of their picnic.

Take a PICNIC CARD from your LUNCHBOX. Now go to 42.

The cave grew darker and darker as they walked further and further in. 'Ooh, listen to that horrible dripping sound,' said Anne as the drips made a loud eerie echo. They had only gone a few steps more when Julian noticed a message painted in large white letters on the cave roof. It began, *IF YOU SEEK THE TREASURE* . . . but the rest of it was in some sort of code. Their hands trembling with excitement, they started to undo their rucksacks so they could consult their codebooks!

Use your CODEBOOK CARD to find out what the message

said by decoding the instruction below. If you don't have one, go to 43 instead.

+F
YPMDC

28

'Are you sure it's worthwhile counting these paces?' Dick asked when there were only a few more to go. 'There's quite clearly not a soul anywhere near here!' The others said that having counted this many, though, they might as well finish. 'Well, I hardly think someone's suddenly going to appear from nowhere,' Dick re-marked awkwardly – but that's exactly what they did do! For the last of the paces took them up to a small nook in the cliffs and sitting in that nook, contentedly smoking his pipe, was an old man with a beard. The Five asked him if he was Jeremiah Boogle and, if so, could they borrow his rowing-boat. The answer was *yes* to both! **Go to 10.**

29

They were still feeling for their torches in their rucksacks when the stairway suddenly became a lot brighter! 'Look, there's a ray of sun coming in through that deep-set window up there,' said Dick, pointing above. They therefore decided they did not need their torches but the stairway still did not prove light enough for Anne to see that there was a pebble lying on the next but one step. She lost her footing, dropping her lunchbox as she did so! 'I'm afraid it sounds like you've smashed your ginger beer bottle,' said Julian, hearing glass breaking.

Take a PICNIC CARD from your LUNCHBOX. Now go to 12.

30

Julian led the way into the shaft – carrying Timmy in his rucksack! It was the only way he could think of to get him down the rungs. He had to descend very slowly because Timmy was such a weight on his back and every so often he took a rest. It was during one of these rests that he suddenly noticed a message on the shaft wall. *MEASURE EXACTLY 30 METRES STRAIGHT DOWN*, it read.

Use your MEASURE CARD to measure these thirty metres – then follow the instruction there. If you don't have one in your RUCKSACK, you'll have to guess which instruction to follow.

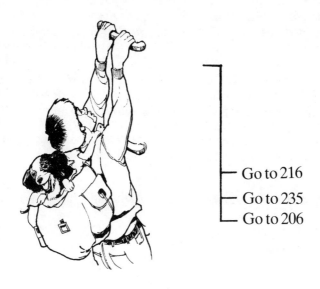

Go to 216
Go to 235
Go to 206

31

The Five finally reached the bottom of the shaft. 'Phew, what a weight you are, Timmy!' Julian said over his shoulder as the others helped the dog out of his rucksack (this had been their clever way of getting him down!). They now investigated the bottom of the shaft, finding that there was a sort of narrow tunnel that led off from it! 'I wonder what that strange swirling noise above is?' Dick asked as they followed the tunnel along. Then he suddenly realised. It was the sea – the tunnel led under the sea! *Go to 300.*

'It's a good idea, George,' Julian said rather doubtfully. 'But I'm not sure our torches will be bright enough to carry all the way to the police station. If only we had something that was a bit stronger!' Then he gave a glance at the huge lamp! He immediately went to his rucksack for a box of matches he had there and, having struck one of the matches, held it to the lamp's wick. For a long while nothing happened but then the wick suddenly caught and the lamp was soon a dazzling white! 'What luck – there's still some oil in it!' George cried and, to celebrate Julian's success, she handed everyone a slice of her cake.

Take a PICNIC CARD from your LUNCHBOX. Now go to 117. (Remember: when there are no picnic cards left in your lunchbox the game is over, and you must start again.)

'Right, who wants to stay here and hold the end?' Julian asked when he was ready with his measuring tape. There was an absolute silence, though – *no one* wanting to stay! 'OK, I'll stay myself,' Julian offered casually, trying to pretend he didn't mind! *Go to 195.*

The children had had to use their torches so much on this adventure, however, that not a single one of them worked any more! 'I'm afraid all our batteries have run down,' Julian told the sergeant regretfully. 'We'll just have to try and make our way up the steps in the dark!' So they all climbed very slowly and carefully but about halfway up George suddenly slipped and crashed to the ground. Although she was all right herself, her ginger beer bottle wasn't. She could hear its broken pieces rattling inside her lunchbox!

Take a PICNIC CARD from your LUNCHBOX. Now go to 217.

As they were feeling through their rucksacks for their torches, however, the whole place suddenly lightened up! The gang had lit a series of small fires near the bridge so the plane would know where to land. 'We won't be requiring those torches of yours after all,' the sergeant told the children quietly. 'We can see all we want now!' There was still no sign of the plane, however, and George shared out the last of her sandwiches to help pass the time.

Take a PICNIC CARD from your LUNCHBOX. Now go to 134. (Remember: when there are no picnic cards left in your lunchbox the game is over, and you must start again.)

'So it's all agreed that Anne's idea sounds best?' Julian asked after their quick discussion. 'That's to go and look at that signpost over there and see if that leads to Wailing Lighthouse.' When they reached the signpost, however, it was difficult to tell *where* it pointed. That was because the writing on it was in some sort of code! 'It looks like a job for our codebooks,' said Dick, beginning to search for his in his rucksack.

Do you have a CODEBOOK in your RUCKSACK? If so, use it

to find out what the signpost said by decoding the instruction below. *(Remember to put it back in your RUCKSACK afterwards.)* **If you don't have a CODEBOOK CARD, go to 84 instead.**

37

Much to the others' surprise, *Anne* volunteered to walk at the front. She'd decided that at least that way she could make sure they didn't go too fast and take any unnecessary risks! They hadn't followed the path along the cliff-tops much further when Julian pointed out a small harbour below. 'Let's look it up on our maps,' he suggested. 'Then we'll know exactly where we are!'

Do you have a MAP in your RUCKSACK? If so, use it to find out which square the harbour is in – then follow the instruction. If you don't have one, you'll have to guess which instruction to follow.

If you think C4	go to 2
If you think B4	go to 22
If you think D4	go to 287

38

Dick and the others decoded the bird-watcher's instructions as: *YOUR SHORTEST ROUTE IS TO HEAD IN THE DIRECTION OF THE SUN.* 'I bet he'll have a shock when he sees us walking that way,' Dick chuckled as they all set off. 'I expect he thought that code was uncrackable!' And Dick was perfectly right. As he watched them disappear in the right direction through his binoculars, the bird-watcher scratched his head in surprise! *Go to 200.*

39

The Five hadn't proceeded much further on their journey when Anne suddenly gave a gasp. 'Oh no – look over there!' she cried, pointing to a thick mist rolling in from the direction of the sea. Within minutes they were totally engulfed by the mist and they could no longer see so much as a metre in front. 'Dick . . . George . . . Anne – are you there?' Julian asked, blindly groping around. 'I suggest we all put on our torches so that we can see a bit better.'

Do you have a TORCH in your RUCKSACK? If so, use it to help light up the way by placing exactly over the shape below – then follow the instruction. If you don't have one, go to 87 instead.

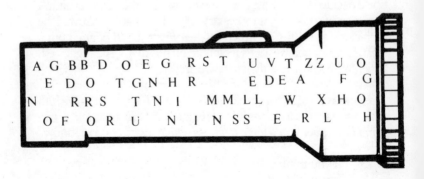

While they were looking for their codebooks, though, Julian made the silly mistake of putting the target on the ground. Suddenly, a gust of wind blew up and lifted the piece of card into the air. Although it soon dropped down again, it was right in the middle of a small marshy area! Timmy was ready to bound in after it but Julian restrained him, saying it might be more dangerous than it looked. To make up for their disappointment at not being able to decode the message, Dick suggested they all have a drink of their ginger beer!

Take a PICNIC CARD from your LUNCHBOX. Now go to 90.

It didn't take much more walking before The Five reached the coastline again, finding themselves at the top of some very high cliffs. And there – just a little further along – was the lighthouse! It stood grey and silent on its little rocky island just out to sea. 'Ooh, doesn't it look eerie,' gulped Anne, as the waves crashed against its base. 'And – listen! – the wind *does* seem to make a wailing noise around it.' The others all shivered as they detected it too but then Julian suddenly diverted their attention. 'Hey, they must be the caves!' he exclaimed, pointing to two large holes in the cliff bottom just opposite the lighthouse. 'Look, that appears to be a path down to them over there. Let's take it!' *Go to 211.*

It was only another ten minutes' walking before The Five reached the coast again, finding themselves high up on the cliffs. And there, standing on a small rocky island just out to sea, was the lighthouse! 'Ooh, doesn't it look eerie,' said Anne as the waves crashed against its sombre silhouette. 'I think I can almost hear its wailing sound as well!' The others started to listen for it too but then Dick suddenly diverted their attention. *Go to 303.*

43

They were just about to start decoding the message on the roof when they heard a sudden chuckle behind them. It nearly made them jump out of their skins! 'Don't go fretting yerselves,' laughed a man with a rather ugly, unshaven face. 'It ain't be no ghost – just me, Ebenezer. An' there's no sense in yer tryin' to decode that there message because it's just someone's joke to deceive folk!' *Go to 110.*

44

They had only counted out seventy of the paces towards the lobster pots when Dick suddenly realised something. 'Oh, how silly we all are!' he said. 'We can *see* that there's no one between here and the lobster pots. This is just a waste of time!' At that very moment, though, an old man with a beard appeared out of a little nook in the cliffs some fifty paces or so ahead. *This* was obviously Jeremiah Boogle! 'There must be some sort of ledge for him to sit on there,' said Dick as they hurried up to him to ask about borrowing his boat. To show their gratitude when Jeremiah said that they could, George gave him a slice of her cake.

Take a PICNIC CARD from your LUNCHBOX. Now go to 10.

Dick suddenly took a deep breath. 'It's all right – *I'll* go first!' he said bravely as he stepped through the door to the lighthouse's dark inside. He immediately found himself at the bottom of a spiral stairway and he led the way up towards the top. He had only climbed about a dozen of the stone steps, however, when he noticed a message chalked at his feet. It read: *BEWARE 40 METRES ON!* He told the others that one of them had better take out their measuring tape!

Use your MEASURE CARD to measure these forty metres – then follow the instruction there. If you don't have a MEASURE in your RUCKSACK, you'll have to guess which instruction to follow.

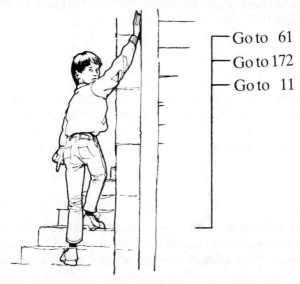

Go to 61
Go to 172
Go to 11

46

'I think I might be on to the treasure at last!' Julian cried excitedly when he had decoded the message on the bell's dusty surface. 'There's an instruction here to look behind the oil cans in the corner!' All walking over to the oil cans, however, they only found an old measuring tape there. 'Well, it's not *too* disappointing,' Dick tried to console them. 'The measuring tape might have been put here to *help* in the search for the treasure. That would mean that it's somewhere near!'

If you don't already have it, put the MEASURE CARD into your RUCKSACK. Now go to 158.

47

'It must be this stack of stones here,' said Dick, showing it to the others on his map. 'They're about the right direction anyway. Now what does it say underneath? Prehistoric pillar. So that's what it is – some sort of monument built in the Stone Age!' *Go to 158.*

48

George had only led them twenty or so rungs down the shaft when she noticed a coded message chalked on to the rock. Unfortunately, her codebook was in her rucksack on her back and it was impossible for her to reach it. She therefore called up to Dick, who was just behind, and asked him to try and get it out for her.

*Use your **CODEBOOK CARD** to find out what the chalked message said by decoding the instruction below. If you don't have a **CODEBOOK** in your **RUCKSACK**, go to 242 instead.*

49

By the time one of them had produced a codebook for Julian, it was too late. The candle's flame had melted the top part of the message away! 'Oh well, at least we can use the candle to see where we're going,' remarked Dick. 'It will save on our torch batteries for a while.' George prepared to lead the way again but, before she did, she suggested they all have a quick sandwich. Her tummy felt as if it hadn't been fed for days!

*Take a **PICNIC CARD** from your **LUNCHBOX**. Now go to 207.*

Their maps showed that the picnic site *was* on the way to the stone bridge. 'So it looks like they *are* the treasure looters we heard!' Dick remarked soberly. 'That explains the boxes they're carrying. Look – you can just about make them out in their arms!' It was a pity they couldn't make out their faces as well though. Then they would have been able to give a description of the men to the police! **Go to 117.**

As soon as they had reached the top of the cliffs, the sergeant hurriedly led the way inland towards the bridge. They at last spotted it ahead – and they spotted several shadowy figures moving about on it too! They all crept a bit nearer – and then the sergeant made them hide behind some large boulders. 'We'll wait here until the plane arrives,' he whispered tensely. 'I want to catch the pilot too!' He asked the children if one of them could lend him a torch, saying he might as well write up a few notes about the case while they were waiting.

Use your TORCH CARD to help the sergeant see by placing exactly over the shape below – then follow the instruction. If you don't have a TORCH in your RUCKSACK, go to 162 instead.

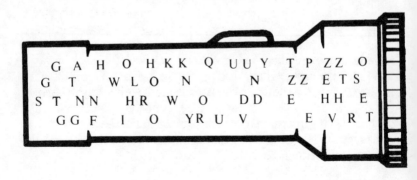

The children were just about to start measuring the seventy metres from the first-aid hut when they suddenly realised that they didn't know *in which direction* to measure. 'We can't go and disturb the Professor again!' exclaimed Julian, scratching his head. 'I wonder what we should do.' While he and the other children were still wondering, however, Timmy trotted off and found a rough footpath. 'Oh, well done, Timmy!' remarked George. 'For being so clever, you can have one of my slices of cherry cake.'

Take a *PICNIC CARD* from your *LUNCHBOX*. Now go to 199.

53

'Perhaps it's time we checked we're going in the right direction,' Julian proposed after about another half hour of walking. The footpath they'd been following had become very unclear and they weren't sure whether they were still on it or not. All of a sudden Anne spotted a man with a pair of binoculars – presumably a bird-watcher – a short distance to their right and she suggested one of them go and ask him.

Throw the *FAMOUS FIVE DICE* to decide which one it's to be.

JULIAN thrown	go to 21
DICK thrown	go to 305
GEORGE thrown	go to 70
ANNE thrown	go to 210
TIMMY thrown	go to 188
MYSTERY thrown	go to 259

'This must be the footpath the coastguard meant!' Julian remarked, when the eighty paces brought them to a narrow path cut into the rocky ground. 'It looks as if it was once some sort of sheep track.' Taking this path, they found that it still followed the line of the cliffs but it ran much further from the edge. 'And it still gives glimpses of the sea every so often,' Julian reassured them, 'so there shouldn't be any worry about missing the lighthouse!' *Go to 2.*

'This must be it!' said George as she found a statue on her map. The map gave the statue's name as Admiral Herbert Woodcock and, just to make sure it was the right one, she looked to see if that name appeared on the statue itself. 'Yes, *Admiral Herbert Woodcock,*' she read delightedly, finding a small plaque at the statue's feet. 'This is it all right!' They now put their maps away again and took the branch of the path that went inland. *Go to 191.*

Flicking through their codebooks, they finally decoded the message as: *WHEN WE'VE FOUND ALL THE TREASURE, WE'LL SECRETLY TAKE IT AWAY TO FRANCE.* 'Gosh,' exclaimed Julian, 'it looks like there is treasure round here after all – and that some gang intends to steal it!' He added that these old paper targets were obviously being used by the gang to pass messages between each other. *Go to 90.*

'Here is the pothole – just in front!' said Dick when they had measured the distance from the sign. After they had put their measuring tapes back in their rucksacks, they all walked carefully round the hole. They had only gone a few steps further, however, when they reached another pothole – one the sign hadn't mentioned! Fortunately, this wasn't such a wide one but it was still big enough to cause Anne to trip. 'Oh no,' she sighed as she dusted herself down, 'I can hear the sound of broken glass from my lunchbox. My bottle of ginger beer must have broken!'

Take a PICNIC CARD from your LUNCHBOX. Now go to 284.

'Here are the steps!' Dick exclaimed with delight when they had measured the ninety metres from the old signpost. They were cut into the face of the cliff and dropped very steeply. Because the steps were so steep, The Five descended them very slowly but at last they reached the cliff bottom. 'Phew, I'm glad that's over!' sighed George with relief. 'I feel quite dizzy!' *Go to 275.*

Probably because she was the most excited, *Anne* reached Jeremiah Boogle's cottage first! For a small payment, Jeremiah was happy to lend them his boat and they were soon rowing it towards the little rocky island on which the lighthouse stood. They were nearly halfway there when Julian's oar scooped up a scrap of paper from the water. He was about to shake it off but then he suddenly noticed some sort of coded message on it!

Use your CODEBOOK CARD to find out what the message said by decoding the instruction below. If you don't have one, go to 126 instead.

60

Anne found the room so dusty that she thought she'd leave looking for the codebooks to the others while she had a quick drink of her ginger beer. Just as she was putting the bottle to her lips, however, it slipped out of her hand and smashed on the floor. Not only was that the end of her ginger beer but it was the end of the chalked message as well. For the drink had spilt right over it and washed it all off!

Take a PICNIC CARD from your LUNCHBOX. Now go to 12.

61

So that no one had to stay behind to keep hold of the end of the measuring tape, Anne had the clever idea of leaving her lunchbox there with the end of the measure shut inside. Unfortunately, though, the box wasn't quite as heavy as they thought and they unknowingly pulled it up some of the steps with them. As a result, they reached forty metres earlier than the tape indicated and were quite unprepared for the loose step there! Dick stumbling on it and receiving a nasty bruise on his knee wasn't the only mishap caused. When they pulled Anne's lunchbox up the rest of the steps, they found that all the jolting had broken her ginger beer bottle!

Take a PICNIC CARD from your LUNCHBOX. Now go to 94.

62

Their search of the room finished, The Five continued up the spiral stairs again, exploring several other small rooms on the way. At last they arrived at the lamp-room at the very top – where the light actually flashed from! There was a balcony running all the way round the outside and they found a small door which led on to it. Trying to shield their eyes from the fierce wind, they suddenly noticed someone flashing a torch at them from the shore. 'It's

Ebenezer!' exclaimed Julian. 'He's flashing in Morse code to us to ask if we've had any luck yet in finding the treasure.' They immediately went to their rucksacks for their own torches so they could reply!

*Use your **TORCH CARD** to flash back this reply by placing exactly over the shape below – then follow the instruction. If you don't have a **TORCH** in your **RUCKSACK**, go to 81 instead.*

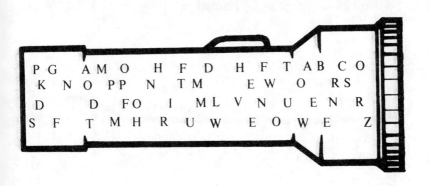

```
P G   A M O   H  F  D   H  F  T A B  C O
  K  N  O  PP   N   TM      E W    O    R S
  D      D   FO   I   ML  V  N  U   E   N R
S  F   T   M H R  U W    E  O  W  E       Z
```

63

After Dick had passed her down her codebook, Anne eagerly started to decode the message on the rock. It finally worked out as: *CLIMB DOWN ANOTHER TWELVE RUNGS AND YOU WILL FIND SOMETHING TO ASSIST YOU.* It became darker and darker as she descended and, by the time she had reached the twelfth rung, she could barely see at all! Feeling around, though, she suddenly located a small hole in the rock. Inside that hole was a torch! 'Just what we needed,' she shouted back to the others as she switched it on. 'It saves us the difficult problem of trying to get out our own!'

*If you don't already have it, put the **TORCH CARD** into your **RUCKSACK**. Now go to 31.*

Timmy was eager to lead the way along the tunnel but he hadn't trotted far when Julian called him back. 'Wait a minute, ol' boy,' he said. 'We're going to have to take out one of our torches first!' They had been able to save their torches until then because there was just enough light coming down the shaft for them to be able to see. The tunnel itself, however, was pitch black!

*Use your **TORCH CARD** to light up the tunnel by placing exactly over the shape below – then follow the instruction. If you don't have one, go to 285 instead.*

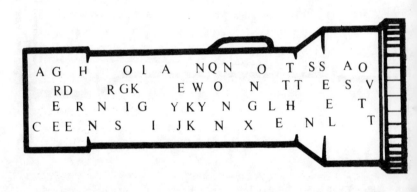

The Five carefully counted the 160 paces from the seventh hole but they found that there was nothing there! 'All I can see is grass,' remarked Dick, baffled. 'I wonder if we didn't count properly – or we didn't make our paces big enough.' But then Anne noticed that it wasn't flag number ten they had been walking towards, as the message instructed, but flag number twelve! So they had to go back to the seventh hole and start all over again! ***Go to 180.***

Julian said they could look up on their maps later, though. The most important thing just at the moment was to try and find a way out so they could inform the police about the gang! 'But how are we going to get past all these boulders?' Anne asked him. 'They're much too heavy for us to move!' Julian agreed, saying their best bet was probably to return to the lighthouse and have another go at that locked door. So he hurriedly led the way back along the tunnel. He was in a bit *too* much of a hurry, though, because he suddenly tripped, dropping his lunchbox. The sound of tinkling glass from inside gave the sad news that his ginger beer bottle was broken!

Take a *PICNIC CARD* from your *LUNCHBOX*. Now go to 196.

The sergeant spotted the cliff steps first himself, immediately ordering the police boat's pilot to land. They all leapt down on to the beach and then hurried towards the steps. They had nearly reached the top when Anne spotted a French banknote fluttering around at her feet. Taking a closer look at it, she noticed that there was a coded message scribbled across it. She told the others to wait a moment while she got out her codebook!

Use your CODEBOOK CARD to work out what the message said by decoding the instruction below. If you don't have a CODEBOOK in your RUCKSACK, go to 147 instead.

Just as the sergeant was about to rip the mask off the man's face, however, he suddenly broke free and ran towards the plane. The sergeant chased after him but it was too late – the pilot pulled the man in and revved up the engine. A moment or two later, the plane had taken off and disappeared into the night. 'Well, at least we've caught all the others,' the sergeant told the children, not too disappointedly, as he brushed himself down. 'And I dare say their leader will be back in this country some day. When he is – I assure you – he won't remain free for long!'

Your adventure wasn't quite successful. If you would like another attempt at solving the mystery, you must start the game again from paragraph one. Try choosing a different EQUIP-MENT CARD this time to see if it gives you any more luck.

69

The children were soon agreed that Dick's idea sounded best – quite simply, just to consult their maps! So they all took their maps out of their rucksacks, trying to find the lighthouse. 'Here it is,' said Dick, pointing to the top corner of his map. 'Now to find where we are at the moment – Kirrin Bay.' George said Kirrin Bay should be easy to find because it was the only sandy bay in the area and there was a small island just opposite, with a ruined castle.

Do you have a MAP in your RUCKSACK? If so, use it to find out which square Kirrin Bay is in – then follow the instruction. (Remember to put the MAP back in your RUCKSACK after-wards.) If you don't have one, you'll have to guess which instruction to follow.

If you think A4	go to 218
If you think B4	go to 20
If you think A3	go to 131

The others didn't have to wait long before George was on her way back from the bird-watcher. 'He wrote down how to get to Wailing Lighthouse on this scrap of paper for me,' she called, brandishing it in the air. She carelessly let it slip from her fingers, though, and the wind blew it along the ground. 'It's disappeared into that pill-box over there!' Julian cried as they all chased after it. It looked so dark and spooky inside the little concrete building that they decided they would only go in with the help of their torches.

Do you have a TORCH in your RUCKSACK? If so, use it to light up the inside of the pill-box by placing exactly over the shape below – then follow the instruction that appears. If you don't have one, go to 86 instead.

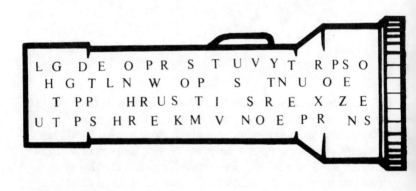

Dick said there wasn't much point in using their torches, though, because even if they did find out what the thing was they wouldn't be able to reach it. The hole was much too deep! 'Anyway, I'm sure it's not part of the treasure or anything,' he added. 'It's probably just an old piece of metal that's fallen down there!' *Go to 137.*

72

They were just taking out their codebooks when Dick actually *spotted* what must have been Wailing Lighthouse in the distance! Its red and white top was just showing above a sharp dip in the land. 'Look, this inland footpath *would* be a short cut to it,' he remarked excitedly. 'We needn't go all the way round the cliffs after all!' They were so impatient to set off along the short cut that they decided just to put their codebooks away again and forget the message on the rock. In spite of their hurry, though, Dick still found time to have a quick swig of his ginger beer on the way!

Take one PICNIC CARD from your LUNCHBOX. Now go to 191.

73

Measuring the seventy metres from the upright rock they at first couldn't find anything but then Timmy started to dig away at some loose stones. 'Oh clever boy, Timmy!' they all praised him as he finally reached a shabby little book wrapped up in a polythene bag. Quickly looking through it, they saw it was a codebook and that it contained some extra codes to the ones in their books, so they decided to take it with them! They somehow felt that it might well help them in their search for the treasure later on.

If you don't already have it, put the CODEBOOK CARD into your RUCKSACK. Now go to 41.

By making Timmy run right across the path of the boys, *George* just reached the youth hostel door first! 'Oh, you cheat, George!' Dick chuckled. 'Timmy forced us to slow right down!' When they had all recovered their breath, they entered the youth hostel. But, instead of there being a warden inside as they'd hoped, it was completely deserted. It was so dark in there that Dick suddenly tripped on a loose floorboard and dropped his lunchbox. They heard the lid click open and his ginger beer bottle roll across the floor. It would need their torches to find it again!

Use your TORCH CARD to light up the youth hostel's floor by placing exactly over the shape below, then follow the instruction. If you don't have one, go to 220 instead.

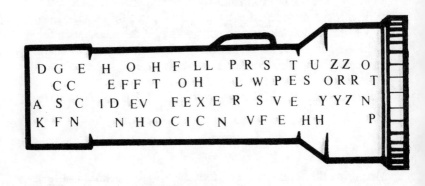

'Only another metre to go . . .' Julian read off his tape as they measured the thirty metres from the sign. 'That means the pothole should be coming up any moment now. Watch where you tread!' They all felt around with their feet, edging very carefully forward. 'Here it is!' George suddenly exclaimed. 'Right in front of me. I don't think it's large enough to fall into but you'd better all give it a wide berth in case you twist your ankle on it!' *Go to 284.*

'It's obviously this part here!' said George, pointing to the bottom corner of her map. It showed some cliffs and a shipwreck just out to sea – exactly as in the photograph. 'I wonder if that's one of the wrecked ships from which the treasure was stolen,' Julian said thoughtfully. 'If it is, it suggests the person who took this photograph is also trying to track down the treasure's whereabouts!' When Timmy suddenly spotted a small codebook near where the photograph had been, they became even more intrigued!

If you don't already have it, put the CODEBOOK CARD into your RUCKSACK. Now go to 27.

Just a fraction ahead of the others, *Dick* reached Jeremiah Boogle's cottage first. He gave a knock on the small wooden door, waiting for someone to answer. 'What ye be wanting with Jeremiah Boogle?' asked a man with an old, crumpled face and a white beard. When

Dick said that they would like to borrow his rowing-boat, he told them that it would cost fifty pence. Dick immediately gave him the fifty pence, asking where the boat was. 'Ye'll find it 110 paces in the direction of my finger!' the old man told them, pointing along the bay.

Use your MEASURE CARD to measure the 110 paces from Jeremiah Boogle – then follow the instruction there. If you don't have a MEASURE in your RUCKSACK, you'll have to guess which instruction to follow.

Go to 184

Go to 10

Go to 222

'This is it!' said George, the first to find the old mill on her map. 'It looks so unimportant, doesn't it? Who would have thought it was once a wicked gang's secret meeting place!' Putting their maps away again, they continued to climb the steps but they had only gone a couple of twists more when Anne made them stop. 'Watch out,' she warned, 'there's something on the step!' She bent down to pick it up. 'Gosh, it's a torch,' she exclaimed. 'Look – it works too!' Partly so they didn't trip on it when they came down again, and partly because they thought it might be useful as a spare, they took it with them!

If you don't already have it, put the TORCH CARD into your RUCKSACK. Now go to 94.

Julian suggested they all try ramming the locked door to see if they could force it open but it remained absolutely fast. As they rubbed their sore shoulders, George suddenly noticed Timmy sniffing at a large iron ring in the stone floor. 'Quick, come over here!' she called to the others when she had gone to have a look at it. 'Timmy's found some sort of trap-door!' They all heaved at the ring, revealing a long vertical shaft with iron rungs down its side. 'Let's go down it,' said Julian excitedly. 'With any luck, it might lead to the outside of the lighthouse!'

Throw the FAMOUS FIVE DICE to decide who is to climb down the shaft first.

JULIAN thrown	go to 30
DICK thrown	go to 174
GEORGE thrown	go to 48
ANNE thrown	go to 143
TIMMY thrown	go to 254
MYSTERY thrown	go to 95

Julian hadn't led them far along the tunnel when he stopped, hearing a faint swirling noise above. 'I was right!' he exclaimed. 'This tunnel *does* lead under the sea. Listen – that's what that sound is!' Knowing that the sea was just above their heads made them all feel rather uncomfortable, however, and they insisted that Julian should keep going. It wasn't long before he stopped again, though, spotting a chalked message on the tunnel's rocky wall. It read: *SEARCH HOLE IN WALL EXACTLY 80 METRES FURTHER ON!* He immediately went to his rucksack for his measuring tape!

Use your MEASURE CARD to measure these eighty metres – then follow the instruction there. If you don't have a MEASURE in your RUCKSACK, you'll have to guess which instruction to follow.

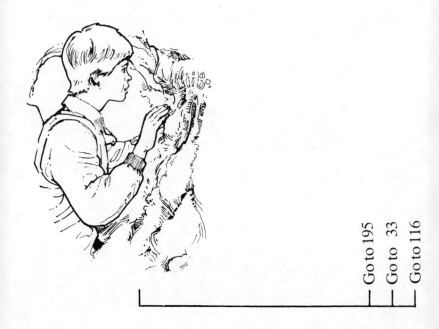

Go to 195

Go to 33

Go to 116

Dick was in such a hurry to get to his rucksack that he accidentally let his lunchbox drop. It slid towards the edge of the balcony, just managing to slip through a gap in the bars! 'Oh no!' he cried as he helplessly watched it fall towards the sea far below. It was such a while before they all recovered from this that, by the time they were ready with their torches, Ebenezer was gone. 'He must have assumed we didn't know Morse code,' Julian said disappointedly.

Take a PICNIC CARD from your LUNCHBOX. Now go to 158. (Remember: when there are no picnic cards left in your lunchbox, the game is over and you must start again.)

82

'There only seems to be the one tall chimney in this area,' said Dick, pointing to his map. 'And that's this one – belonging to a copper mine.' His map showed that the copper mine was in a south-westerly direction from the lighthouse and so it was south-west that their window must have been facing! *Go to 12.*

83

'There are the steps!' Dick suddenly cried, peering through the darkness. 'About another fifty metres further along!' As the police boat quickly came ashore they all leapt out on to the pebbles, running towards the steps. 'Do any of you children have a torch by any chance?' the sergeant asked just as they were about to climb. 'These steps could be quite dangerous in the dark!'

Use your TORCH CARD to light the steps up by placing exactly over the shape below – then follow the instruction. If you don't have a TORCH in your RUCKSACK, go to 34 instead.

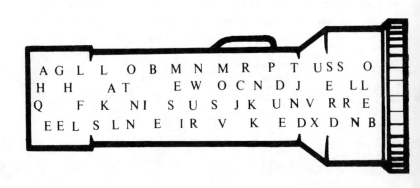

84

Just as Julian, Dick and Anne were about to consult their codebooks, however, George walked round to look at the other side of the signpost. 'Hey, we don't need our codebooks,' she exclaimed. 'This side has a decoded version. And it *does* say Wailing Lighthouse!' So they all put their codebooks away again, following the signpost's direction. *Go to 53.*

85

Dick said *he* would walk at the front to begin with and so he led the way as the narrow path hugged the cliff edge. He hadn't led them far, however, when he suddenly stopped. 'I wish you'd warn us when you're going to stop,' George told him crossly from behind. Dick said that he was sorry but he had stopped suddenly because there was a message written on the path. It was chalked across a flat piece of rock and read: *130 PACES FURTHER ON YOU WILL FIND SOMETHING THAT PROVES USEFUL.* 'Well go on then, Dick,' the others all urged excitedly behind him. 'Start counting the 130 paces!'

Do you have a MEASURE CARD in your RUCKSACK? If so, use it to measure the 130 paces from the message on the rock – then follow the instruction there. If you don't have a MEASURE, you'll have to guess which instruction to follow.

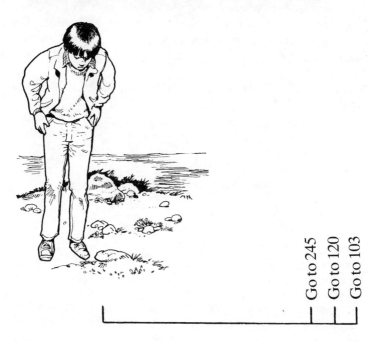

Go to 245

Go to 120

Go to 103

They were just starting to look for their torches in their rucksacks when George suddenly noticed that Timmy was no longer with them. 'He's just disappeared into thin air!' she exclaimed with alarm. 'Oh – where can he be!' They looked all round for him but then he suddenly appeared right in front of them – out of the pill-box! 'Oh look, he's got the bird-watcher's note in his mouth!' George cried with relief as she hugged him. *Go to 200.*

87

They were still feeling around for their torches in their rucksacks when Dick said that maybe they shouldn't use them after all. 'The mist will probably pass over soon,' he told them, 'and we really ought to save our batteries for when we explore the caves.' The others all thought this very sensible and they decided the best thing to do was just to sit where they were. 'To help pass the time,' Anne said, feeling through her lunchbox, 'I suggest we each have a sandwich.' Almost as soon as they had finished their sandwiches, the mist cleared!

Take a PICNIC CARD from your LUNCHBOX. Now go to 191.

88

They were still trying to work out what the bangs might be when Dick spotted a soldier coming from the direction of the ridge. 'Hello,' he shouted to them as he got nearer. 'As you can probably hear, we're out on the range this morning and I just wanted to warn you not to come too close in case there are any stray bullets!' As the soldier then returned towards the ridge, the children all grinned at each other. Of course, that's what the bangs were – they were from an army shooting range! *Go to 41.*

Just as they were looking for the sea-arch on their maps, however, George gave an excited shout. 'We don't need the maps!' she exclaimed, pointing to her left. 'That white thing sticking out over there is the top of the lighthouse!' Running a bit further along the cliffs, they could soon see the whole of it. It stood tall, grey and eerie on its little island of rock just out to sea. To celebrate their discovery, Dick suggested they all have a quick sandwich!

Take a PICNIC CARD from your LUNCHBOX. Now go to 25.
(Remember: when there are no picnic cards left in your lunchbox the game is over, and you must start again.)

90

'Look, there's some sort of farmhouse ahead!' George exclaimed after they'd been trekking across the rough countryside for another quarter of an hour or so. 'Let's go and ask them how much further it is to Wailing Lighthouse.' As they got nearer to the building, though, they realised that it wasn't a farmhouse at all but a youth hostel. They could tell by the flag outside, which had a large green triangle on it. They decided to have a race up to the door!

Throw the FAMOUS FIVE DICE to decide who is to win this race.

JULIAN thrown	go to 263
DICK thrown	go to 182
GEORGE thrown	go to 74
ANNE thrown	go to 289
TIMMY thrown	go to 212
MYSTERY thrown	go to 107

Before they could switch on their torches, however, the mysterious voice came again. 'Don't go alarming yerselves,' it chuckled. 'It don't be no ghost – just me, Ebenezer.' And at that the stranger switched on a lamp so they could see his face. The Five all gave a sigh of relief. It wasn't a very pleasant-looking face, but at least it was human! *Go to 110.*

The Five still had some way to run to the nearest of the cottages when they noticed a small fishing-boat coming ashore. 'Perhaps *that's* Jeremiah Boogle,' Julian suggested, making them all stop. The grey-bearded old man *was* Jeremiah Boogle and, for a small fee, he said he was perfectly happy to lend them his rowing-boat. ''Ere it be,' he told them, as he led them to the back of his ramshackle cottage. 'But mind ye don't take it anywhere near Bell Rocks. The coast be very treach'rous there!' As The Five rowed the little boat out into the sea, they thought they had better look up Bell Rocks on their maps.

Use your MAP to find out which square Bell Rocks is in (where there's a bell on the cliff-tops) – then follow the instruction. If you don't have a MAP in your RUCKSACK, you'll have to guess which instruction to follow.

If you think E4	go to 185
If you think E2	go to 233
If you think E3	go to 140

The children were still discussing who should enter the lighthouse first when they suddenly noticed that Timmy was missing! A moment later, however, they heard his bark from inside! They went through the entrance after him, finding themselves at the bottom of a spiral stone staircase. They started to climb it, following it round and round until they reached a small room about halfway up. 'I wonder what this was for?' asked Julian – but the room was so dark that they were only likely to find out with the help of their torches.

Use your TORCH CARD to light up the room by placing exactly over the shape below – then follow the instruction. If you don't have a TORCH in your RUCKSACK, go to 266 instead.

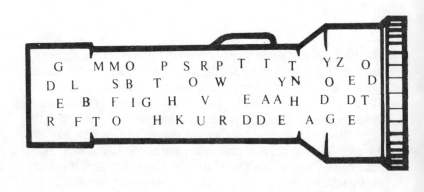

94

After passing through and exploring the lighthouse's storeroom, oil-room and living-room, the Five finally came to the lamp-room at the very top of the stone steps. The huge lamp took up half the floor and there was glass all the way round the room so that it could easily be seen. 'Look, there's a bell here as well,' said Julian. 'It must have been a back-up in case the lamp wouldn't light.' Walking over to the massive bell, he noticed that there was a coded message written in the thick dust on its surface. He immediately went to his rucksack for his codebook!

Use your CODEBOOK CARD to find out what the message said by decoding the instruction below. If you don't have a CODEBOOK in your RUCKSACK, go to 226 instead.

Julian was just about to lead the way down the shaft when Anne had a closer look at the trap-door's iron ring. Scratched on its surface was a tiny coded message! She told Julian to wait a moment while she got out her codebook.

*Use your **CODEBOOK CARD** to find out what the message on the ring said by decoding the instruction below. If you don't have a **CODEBOOK** in your **RUCKSACK**, go to 274 instead.*

As the children were looking for their maps, however, the sergeant noticed a number of small fires in the distance. He tried to think what they might be and then he suddenly realised. 'Of course!' he exclaimed, 'they're to show the plane where to land! Hurry everybody – the bridge is in *this* direction!' Finally approaching the fires – and spotting several shadowy figures there – the sergeant quickly made them all hide behind some large boulders. 'We'll wait here until the gang's plane arrives,' he whispered to his constables. The wait made them so tense that George munched her way through the remainder of her sandwiches!

Take a PICNIC CARD from your LUNCHBOX. Now go to 134. (Remember: when there are no picnic cards left in your lunchbox the game is over, and you must start again.)

97

'The hole should be coming up any moment now,' Dick called back from the front as they nearly reached the seventy-metre mark on the measuring tape. 'Be ready to grab me in case I suddenly fall in!' Dick managed to spot the hole, though, and safely jumped to the other side. He then helped the others across – although George insisted on doing it by herself! She just managed to make it, finding the hole wider than she thought. She was a little shaken but Dick wasn't at all sympathetic. 'That serves you right for trying to be so clever!' he told her. *Go to 207.*

98

The others had still to open their maps when Dick said that they needn't bother. Looking beyond the picnic site, he suddenly spotted the stone bridge! 'So they *are* heading in that direction!' he exclaimed. 'What a pity they're too far away for us to see their faces. We're just going to have to hope the police hurry up and notice our signal so the gang can be stopped before their plane arrives!' Everyone was making themselves so anxious about it that George handed round her sandwiches to try and relax them.

Take a PICNIC CARD from your LUNCHBOX. Now go to 117. (Remember: when there are no picnic cards left in your lunchbox the game has to stop, and you must start again.)

They finally approached the stone bridge, noticing several shadowy figures standing on it. The sergeant quickly made them all crouch behind some boulders! 'I don't want us to do anything until the plane arrives,' the sergeant told his constables in a tense whisper. 'That way, we'll catch the pilot as well. So we'll just stay here and wait!' As they were waiting, their throats dry with suspense, the sergeant asked the children if they could take out their torches, ready for when the plane arrived.

Use your TORCH CARD to carry out this request by placing exactly over the shape below – then follow the instruction. If you don't have a TORCH in your RUCKSACK, go to 35 instead.

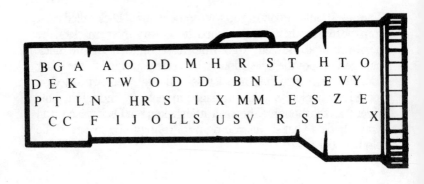

100

'This must be the footpath to Sharprock Cliffs,' said Julian when they had measured the seventy metres from the first-aid hut. He was pointing to a narrow track just back from the beach. They immediately started to follow it but they hadn't gone far when Dick spotted a map at their feet. 'Someone must have dropped it,' he remarked as he picked it up. 'I know we already each have a map but perhaps we ought to take this one as a spare in case anyone loses theirs.'

If you don't already have it, put the MAP into your RUCK-SACK. Now go to 199.

101

Just as George was about to start flashing the Morse code signal with her torch, however, the lifeboat suddenly made a sharp turn and sped out to sea. 'It must have just received a distress call,' said Dick. 'There's no point in trying to send your signal now, George!' As they continued along the footpath, they all hoped that the person in distress would be saved. 'I'm sure he will be,' said George cheerfully. 'That lifeboat captain is one of the best there is!' *Go to 2.*

102

Always keen to play the leader, *George* insisted on walking at the front. The footpath seemed to inch nearer and nearer the cliff edge and Anne covered up her eyes as she saw George suddenly stoop. She thought she was about to fall over the edge but, instead of the distant splash she'd expected, she just heard George laughing. 'Don't worry,' she chuckled. 'I'd simply bent down to pick up this old coin I'd spotted. I'm sure it's gold!' On examining the coin more closely, they all noticed some sort of coded message scratched across it and they quickly opened their rucksacks for their codebooks.

Do you have a CODEBOOK CARD in your RUCKSACK? If so, use it to find out what the inscription on the coin said by decoding the instruction below. If you don't have one, go to 269 instead.

103

Finally reaching 130 paces from the message, Dick scratched his head. 'There's absolutely nothing here – useful or otherwise!' he remarked, searching all round his feet. Julian said someone before them must have picked up whatever it was. 'No doubt the person for whom the message was actually intended,' he guessed. 'I wonder who it was.' *Go to 137.*

When Dick insisted that he *was* perfectly sensible, the bird-watcher scribbled something down on a piece of paper. 'Well, let's just see, shall we?' he replied sourly. 'Here's the direction for Wailing Lighthouse written in a special code. If you *are* a sensible person, as you say, then you should have no trouble working it out!' As Dick ran back with the piece of paper towards the others, he told himself it was a good job they each had codebooks with them!

Do you have a CODEBOOK in your RUCKSACK? If so, use it to find out what the piece of paper said by decoding the instruction below. If you don't have one, go to 149 instead.

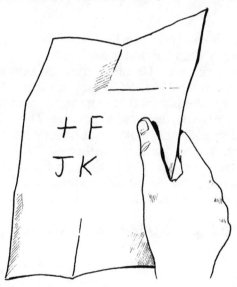

Locating the golf course on their maps, they saw that they were still going the right direction for Wailing Lighthouse after all! 'Why do golfers always shout "fore" before they hit the ball?' Anne asked as they continued walking. Julian said that it was to warn other people, because a flying ball could be very dangerous. ***Go to 39.***

106

'There's no codebook anywhere round here,' Dick remarked bewilderedly when they had finally measured the seventy metres from the upright rock. He turned over a few loose stones with his foot but still without luck. 'Maybe the problem is that we haven't got the right direction for the firing range,' Julian suggested. 'All we've got to go on is the sound of the bangs. They might just be an echo and misleading us!' So they tried measuring the seventy metres in a totally different direction from the rock. 'Well, we can't search round here all day,' said Dick when this still proved unsuccessful. After refreshing themselves with a sandwich, therefore, they left the spot and continued on their way.

Take a PICNIC CARD from your LUNCHBOX. Now go to 41.

107

They were all about halfway to the youth hostel door when a man with a rather mean-looking face emerged from it. 'There's no point in running,' he shouted at them. 'This youth hostel ain't open any more for people to stay!' Julian told him that they didn't wish to stay, but merely to enquire how much further it was to Wailing Lighthouse. 'Never 'eard of it. Now be off with you!' the man snapped as he disappeared into the building again with a slam of the door. Rather resentfully, the children did start to leave but as they were passing the youth hostel flagpole, Anne noticed a message carved down its base! It was in code, though, and so they would need their codebooks!

Use your CODEBOOK CARD to find out what the message said by decoding the instruction below. If you don't have one, go to 203 instead.

108

Measuring the forty metres from the sign, the children found the pothole, stepping carefully round it. 'We're lucky someone put that sign there,' Dick said when they were all safely past. 'I wonder who it was.' Julian replied that it must have been one of those fishermen from the little cottages. 'Which would suggest they have quite a few people coming to the caves looking for the treasure!' he added. *Go to 284.*

'It says that the treasure is within a quarter of a mile!' exclaimed Julian excitedly, as he was the first to decode the message on the oil drum. 'That presumably means we've got to walk that distance into the cave,' he added. As they now began to enter the shadows of the cave, Anne asked anxiously how far a quarter of a mile was. 'Oh, roughly from here to the lighthouse,' Julian replied. *Go to 27.*

Ebenezer told them he knew the caves like the back of his hand, often showing people round, but he had never come across so much as one piece of treasure. 'So I'm afraid yer just be wasting yer time!' he added. When Julian told him that they were determined to keep looking, Ebenezer tried to think how he could help. 'Well, p'rhaps yer best going over to the lighthouse then,' he suggested. 'There's tale that the treasure's really hidden in there!' *Go to 304.*

Measuring the distance along the circular wall, they found that it took them nearly three times round! 'I think this is someone's idea of a joke!' said Dick crossly but then he saw that they had come to a loose brick in the wall. They hadn't noticed it the previous two times they had passed! Dick excitedly pulled the brick out, expecting to see the treasure hidden behind. There was no gold or silver unfortunately – but there was a book of secret codes!

If you don't already have it, put the CODEBOOK CARD into your RUCKSACK. Now go to 62.

112

Julian said they could consult their maps later, though – he wanted to finish this climb as quickly as possible! So they agreed to leave their maps in their rucksacks, continuing up the steps. The stairway soon became so dark, however, that they had to stop again while one of them took out a torch. 'Here you are, we'll use mine,' said George, switching it on – but at that very moment she tripped over Timmy and let her torch drop. 'I'm afraid there's no point in going after it,' said Dick sadly, as they heard it roll and crash all the way to the bottom of the stairs. 'It will be well and truly broken by now!'

If you have one, remove the TORCH CARD from your RUCKSACK. *Now go to 94.*

113

'I've got it!' Julian exclaimed, although keeping his voice to a whisper so the men didn't hear him. 'This undersea tunnel leads back to one of the caves in the cliff. It was probably built as an alternative route into the lighthouse to use when the sea was too rough to cross – but has since been blocked up. Anyway – those men we can hear are in the cave now, looting all the treasure so they can whisk it away by plane!' Dick slapped Julian on the shoulder in congratulation, sure that he was right. 'They said that the plane will be picking them up at a stone bridge, didn't they?' he asked quickly. 'Let's see if we can find it on our maps!'

Use your MAP to find out which square the stone bridge is in – then follow the instruction. If you don't have a MAP in your RUCKSACK, you'll have to guess which instruction to follow.

If you think A1	go to 159
If you think B1	go to 15
If you think B2	go to 66

114

George insisted they take no notice of the message, though – she wanted them to climb down the rungs as quickly as possible and make sure Timmy was all right at the bottom. Hearing the anxiety in her voice, the others agreed. Just before they started moving again, however, George took a sandwich from her lunchbox and dropped it down the shaft. 'That'll be something for Timmy to eat while he's waiting,' she explained.

Take a PICNIC CARD from your LUNCHBOX. Now go to 216.

Always more worried about what might come up from behind than what was in front, *Anne* offered to go first along the tunnel! She wasn't going to start, though, until Dick had passed her his torch (they'd decided only to use one torch at a time in the shaft to save their batteries). Just as she took it from him, however, Dick's torch flickered and went out! They all quickly felt through their rucksacks for another one!

Use your TORCH CARD to light the tunnel up again by placing exactly over the shape below – then follow the instruction. If you don't have a TORCH in your RUCKSACK, go to 243.

```
B G   D E   O   J N   D   A   L L     T   B D D O
  T   W     F J O   I   U N S E   U J R     C D
L     M H   F O   J   I N V  SU   U  N E J   R
T Z   F   N O  I   N P  V S R  E     P R     O
```

Reaching the eighty-metre mark on their measuring tape, they all started searching excitedly for the hole in the wall. At last George discovered it and she put her hand right in, hoping to feel jewels or gold coins. Instead, there was just a torch. They weren't too disappointed, though, because – much to their surprise – they found that it worked! 'It proves that someone else has been along this tunnel recently,' Julian remarked thoughtfully. 'I wonder if he was looking for the treasure?'

If you don't already have it, put the TORCH CARD into your RUCKSACK. Now go to 207.

One . . . two hours had now passed but there was still no response to their signal! 'Oh, surely the police must have seen it by now!' Dick said desperately as he stared into the night. 'Look, it's pitch black out there!' Suddenly, though, he spotted a tiny blue light down below, seeming to come across the water. A minute or two later there was a loud banging at the bottom of the lighthouse and the sound of footsteps rushing up the stairs. The children all gave a cry of relief as a sergeant and several policemen suddenly appeared! *Go to 267.*

Their maps showed that the lighthouse was to the right of Kirrin Bay and so that was the direction they started to walk. 'Now, not too near the edge, Timmy,' George warned her dog as the coastline gradually grew steeper. 'We don't want you falling over!' Seconds later, though, and Timmy seemed to have totally forgotten George's warning, and began sniffing his way right up to the edge. The children were just about to scream at him when he came trotting back to them – with something in his mouth! It was an old measuring tape that he had found in the grass.

If you don't already have it, put the MEASURE CARD into your RUCKSACK. Now go to 199.

'I can't see any footpath,' Dick complained when they had measured the seventy metres from the first-aid hut. The others couldn't find one either but then Anne spotted a slight depression in the grass about another hundred metres or so further in from the beach. 'It's a bit overgrown but it must be the footpath,' she said, leading the others towards it. 'The Professor is probably so absent-minded,' she added, 'that he can't remember whether it was seventy metres from the first-aid hut or *a hundred and* seventy!' To celebrate their discovery of the footpath up to Sharprock Cliffs, they each had a sandwich from their lunchboxes before continuing.

Take a PICNIC CARD from your LUNCHBOX. Now go to 199.

'128 . . . 129 . . . 130!' Dick counted, but he couldn't see anything on the path at that point, useful or otherwise! Then, suddenly, he noticed that one of the flat rocks just in front of his feet was a bit loose. He bent down and prized it out. 'Look, there's a codebook underneath,' he exclaimed. 'This was obviously what the message wanted us to find!' Rather ominously, though, Julian reminded him that it was probably for *someone else* to find!

If you don't already have it, put the CODEBOOK CARD into your RUCKSACK. Now go to 137.

121

'Ah, at least we can just about see where we're walking again!' Dick remarked with relief as they all switched their torches on. George suddenly screamed as her torch's beam picked out what looked like a small pothole just in front of her feet. As they examined it more closely, however, they saw that it wasn't a hole at all but a map that someone had dropped. 'Let's take it with us in case it has got more detail than any of ours,' said Dick, popping it into his rucksack. He had just strapped his rucksack up again when the mist suddenly lifted and they could see perfectly well once more!

If you don't already have it, put the MAP into your RUCK-SACK. Now go to 191.

'Yes, look, I was right,' Julian said as he stabbed a finger at his map. 'There *is* an army shooting range nearby!' They were just about to strap up their rucksacks again when Anne noticed a measuring tape on the ground. 'Which silly person has dropped their measuring tape?' she asked with a chuckle. On checking, though, they found that none of them had – it must have just been lying there! Since a spare could always come in useful, they decided to take it with them.

If you don't already have it, put the MEASURE CARD into your RUCKSACK. Now go to 90.

'Oh, who's scared of a silly old cave!' George remarked breezily and *she* eventually led the way inside. As it grew darker and darker, however, she began to wish she hadn't! 'Ooh – what's that?' she suddenly cried as she saw a slight glow ahead. 'It's not a pair of eyes, is it?' They wondered whether it might be the ghost of one of those drowned sailors but, staring a little harder at it, Dick realised that it was some sort of sign written in luminous paint. As they got nearer, they saw that it read: *DANGEROUS POTHOLE 40 METRES*

FURTHER IN. They decided they had better get out their measuring tapes!

Use your *MEASURE CARD* to measure the forty metres from the message – then follow the instruction there. If you don't have one in your *RUCKSACK*, you'll have to guess which instruction to follow.

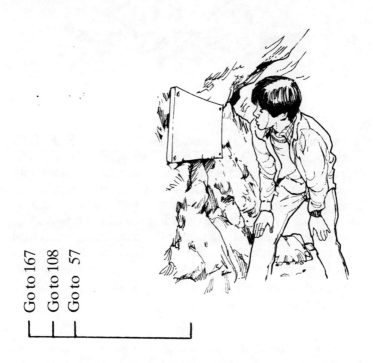

Go to 167
Go to 108
Go to 57

124

'Ah, just what we wanted to know,' exclaimed Julian when he had finished decoding the message on the flagpole. 'It says that the caves opposite Wailing Lighthouse are just over half a mile away!' As they immediately got going again, however, Julian couldn't help feeling a little troubled by this coded message. Who had put it there? And why had they been so secret about it! *Go to 42.*

125

They finally decoded the message as: *IF YOU SEEK THE TREASURE, THEN YOU'D BETTER KEEP LOOKING!* 'It's obviously some sort of mean trick,' said Julian, tutting with annoyance as they put their codebooks away again. 'I wonder who could have written it?' Much to their surprise, Julian was suddenly given an answer by a strange chuckling voice from behind. 'Oh, there be plenty of jokers come to these 'ere caves,' it laughed as a man with a rather ugly, unshaven face came forward. 'Don't worry, I don't be no spook or anything. Me name's Ebenezer!' *Go to 110.*

126

As Anne reached for her rucksack to look for her codebook, however, she suddenly slipped and made the boat rock dangerously. Fortunately they were finally able to steady it but the scrap of paper slithered from Julian's oar as they did so. 'It must have sunk this time,' George sighed after they'd unsuccessfully tried to find it again. Since Anne felt it was all her fault, she gave everyone a drink from her bottle of ginger beer to make up for the loss of the message!

Take a PICNIC CARD from your LUNCHBOX. Now go to 185.

They were still waiting for someone to enter the lighthouse first when George suddenly noticed that Timmy had wandered off. 'Oh, Timmy, be careful,' she shouted, spotting him right at the water's edge. Timmy continued to sniff around the rocks, however, as if he had found something – so George hurried down to investigate. 'Hey, look,' she called back to the others. 'There's a coded message chiselled into one of the rocks. Everyone get out their codebooks!'

Use your CODEBOOK CARD to find out what the message said by decoding the instruction below. If you don't have a CODEBOOK in your RUCKSACK, go to 157 instead.

128

Their hands were shaking with fear so much, however, that they just couldn't get their rucksacks open! 'Oh, why didn't we have our torches out earlier!' exclaimed George, still fiddling with her straps. At last she managed to free them but at that very moment a pair of black and white wings came flapping down, brushing right past their faces. Dick suddenly burst into relieved laughter. 'Why, it was just a puffin!' he chuckled. 'It must have come into the lighthouse through some hole nearer the top. Probably looking for shelter!' **Go to 12.**

129

As soon as Dick had passed down the codebook from the top of her rucksack, George began to decode the chalked message on the rock. 'It says that the shaft goes right down through the lighthouse's foundations and is fifty metres deep,' she called up to the others when she had worked it all out. 'That means we can't even be halfway yet!' **Go to 31.**

130

They were just about to start along the tunnel when Julian sniffed at the air. 'I'm sure I can smell paraffin,' he said. 'I wonder what it's doing down here.' He followed the direction of the smell, soon walking into a small tinny object on the ground. The light coming down the shaft wasn't nearly enough to see the object clearly, however, and so he asked the others to get out one of their torches.

Use your TORCH CARD to light up the tinny object by placing exactly over the shape below – then follow the instruction. If you don't have a TORCH in your RUCKSACK, go to 294 instead.

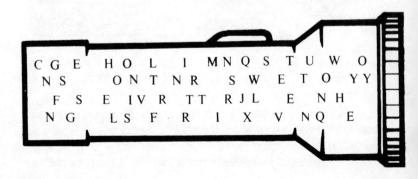

```
C G E    H O L    I   M N Q S   T U  W    O
  N S       O N T N R      S W   E  T O   Y Y
   F S   E  I V R   T T   R J L     E    N H
   N G      L S  F · R   I   X   V  N Q    E
```

'Of course, you know who this island with the ruined castle belongs to, don't you?' George asked conceitedly when they had found Kirrin Bay on their maps. She waited for an answer but the others refused to give her one. 'Oh all right, George!' Julian gave in after a while. 'The island belongs to you, having been in your family for generations and given to you by your mother. Now all *that's* been sorted out, do you think we could possibly get moving again?' *Go to 20.*

'We don't need to consult our maps, silly!' Julian told him, tapping Dick on the head. 'Look, you can just about *see* the stone bridge. It's over there, a mile or so beyond the picnic site!' Following Julian's finger, Dick saw that he was right. There was the stone bridge – in the exact direction the men were heading! They all screwed up their eyes, trying to see what the men looked like so they could give a description to the police, but they were too far away. 'Oh well, let's have something to eat,' Julian suggested disappointedly. 'There's not much else we can do for the moment!'

Take a PICNIC CARD from your LUNCHBOX. Now go to 117. (Remember: when there are no picnic cards left in your lunchbox the game is over, and you must start again.)

'I think that's them,' Julian suddenly exclaimed, pointing to his left. 'Can you see? – about a hunded metres further along.' The others *couldn't* see the steps, though; in fact, they could see nothing but darkness. 'Well, someone pass me a torch,' he suggested. 'Perhaps it will be clearer then!'

Use your TORCH CARD to help light up the steps by placing exactly over the shape below – then follow the instruction. If you don't have a TORCH in your RUCKSACK, go to 301 instead.

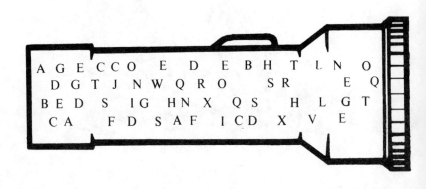

A G E C C O E D E B H T L N O
D G T J N W Q R O S R E Q
B E D S I G H N X Q S H L G T
C A F D S A F I C D X V E

Suddenly, they heard an engine noise above! Staring up into the dark sky, they could just make out a small plane preparing to land. 'It's touching down *now*!' the sergeant told his men as he peeped from behind their boulder. 'As soon as the pilot shows himself, I'm going to give the order to move!' The tension became almost unbearable as they waited but, at last, the sergeant leapt out, rushing towards the gang. 'That looks like the leader of the gang there!' Julian remarked excitedly as they watched the sergeant grab a man with a mask over his face. 'Any second now we should be able to see who he is!'

Use your CODEBOOK to find out by decoding the answer below. If you don't have a CODEBOOK in your RUCKSACK, go to 68 instead.

135

'Hurray, it *does* point to Wailing Lighthouse!' they all cheered as they decoded the writing on the signpost. As they followed its direction, Anne asked why a signpost should be in code. 'Yes, it does seem rather odd, doesn't it?' Julian replied. 'But don't you remember how, when we were looking for the Wrecker's Tower, a lot of the signposts were in code? I expect it's for the same reason – so as few people as possible know the secrets of this part of Cornwall!' *Go to 53.*

136

It was so windy at the top of the stone tower, however, that it was impossible to keep their maps open long enough to read them! Julian therefore suggested they forget about looking up the tower and return to the bottom so they could continue on their journey. 'All that really matters,' he told them encouragingly, as they descended the narrow steps, 'is that we now know the lighthouse's direction again!' *Go to 39.*

137

After another quarter of a mile or so, their footpath reached a statue. It was here that the footpath divided. One branch continued to run along the cliff edge and the other turned more inland. 'We obviously want the one that follows the cliffs,' said Dick but then Anne noticed some directions on the base of the statue. They said that the cliff path should be taken for Wreckage Point, but for Wailing Lighthouse it should be the inland path. 'It must be a short cut to save going round the whole jagged coastline,' remarked Julian. Before they started on the path, George suggested they looked up the statue on their maps to find out where they were.

Use your MAP to find out which square the statue is in – then follow the instruction. If you don't have a MAP in your RUCKSACK, you'll have to guess which instruction to follow.

If you think E4	go to 191
If you think D4	go to 165
If you think C4	go to 55

138

Having found the shooting range on their maps, the children were putting them away again when Anne noticed a light coming from the bottom of her rucksack. 'Oh no,' she cried, clapping her hand to her head, 'I must have left my torch on!' She hoped the batteries hadn't run down too much but, just as she was about to switch the torch off, the light flickered out by itself. The batteries were obviously completely flat!

If you have it, remove the TORCH CARD from your RUCK-SACK. Now go to 41.

139

'Why would anyone want to hide a secret codebook?' Anne asked as they started to measure the seventy metres from the rock. 'Do you think it has anything to do with the treasure in the caves?' Julian said he wasn't sure but it certainly seemed possible! *Go to 106.*

140

'Look – Bell Rocks is right round the next headland,' said George when she was the first to find the cliff-top bell on her map. 'So there's nothing for us to worry about!' They had rowed about halfway to the little rocky island on which the lighthouse stood when Anne felt something roll about under her feet. Reaching down, she found that it was a torch!

If you don't already have it, put the TORCH CARD into your RUCKSACK. Now go to 185.

141

'It works out as: *LIFT UP LOOSE FLOORBOARD NEAR THE WINDOW!*' Julian told the others excitedly when he was the first to decode the chalked message. 'It sounds like the treasure's hidden under *there*!' When they had found the loose floorboard and felt underneath, however, they were disappointed. There wasn't any gold or silver there but just an old map of the area! 'Never mind,' said Dick, putting the map into his rucksack. 'It might come in useful as a spare!'

If you don't already have it, put the MAP into your RUCK-SACK. Now go to 12.

142

Deciding just to use the one torch so they didn't confuse Ebenezer, they flashed back the message that they *hadn't* had any luck yet. Ebenezer then flashed a message to tell them to keep looking and not to get downhearted. They were just about to thank him for this encouragement when he suddenly disappeared from the shore! Nevertheless, the children followed his advice, returning inside to search the lamp-room. They didn't find any treasure there but they *did* find an old map of the area – Julian popping it into his rucksack as a spare!

If you don't already have it, put the MAP into your RUCK-SACK. Now go to 158.

143

Anne volunteered to enter the shaft first, wanting to get out of that horrible lighthouse as soon as possible! She hadn't climbed down far when she noticed a message chiselled into the shaft's rocky side. Unfortunately, it was in code, however, and so it needed her codebook. Since she couldn't reach back to her rucksack for it herself, she asked Dick, who was just above her, to do so.

Use your CODEBOOK CARD to find out what the message

said by decoding the instruction below. If you don't have a
CODEBOOK *in your* **RUCKSACK**, *go to 215 instead.*

$$+ F$$
$$O Z$$

144

As they were slipping off their rucksacks to get to their measuring tapes, however, a couple of bats flew out just in front of them. Dick was so startled that he lost his footing, falling right into the centre of the pebbles! 'Oh no, I've disturbed the message!' he exclaimed. 'And I can't remember how many metres it told us to measure either!' They therefore decided they would just have to estimate the distance to the hole but it came sooner than they expected and Dick found himself falling to the ground for a second time! 'Oh, poor Dick!' George laughed when she saw that he wasn't hurt. 'Have a piece of my cake to cheer you up!'

Take a PICNIC CARD from your LUNCHBOX. Now go to 207.

145

There was a sigh of relief from them all as they at last found another torch and switched it on. 'Let's just hope these batteries don't suddenly run down as well!' said Anne as she started along the tunnel, carrying the torch. The others followed close behind, Julian holding on to the tail of Anne's anorak to reassure her! *Go to 207.*

146

'There they are!' George exclaimed, suddenly spotting the cliff steps through the darkness. As soon as the police motor-boat had stopped, they all jumped out on to the pebbles and hurried towards the steps. They at last reached the top and quickly followed a little footpath that went in the direction of the stone bridge. At least, it *should* have gone in the direction of the bridge – but they suddenly found themselves at a small lake, with several huts around its edge. 'It looks like a bird reserve,' the sergeant said bewilderedly. 'We must have taken a wrong turn somewhere in the dark!' He asked the children to look up the bird reserve on their maps so they would know where they were.

Use your MAP to find out which square the bird reserve is in – then follow the instruction. If you don't have a MAP in your RUCKSACK, you'll have to guess which instruction to follow.

If you think A2	go to 246
If you think C2	go to 276
If you think B2	go to 208

147

The sergeant told Anne that there wasn't really time to decode the message, though. They needed every second they had or they wouldn't reach the bridge before the gang's plane did! So they all hurriedly continued up the steps but they had only gone up a few more when George tripped over Timmy and dropped her lunchbox. Fortunately, Julian was just behind her and he was able to stop the lunchbox with his foot before it rolled all the way to the cliff bottom. Unfortunately, though, he could hear that George's ginger beer bottle was broken!

Take a PICNIC CARD from your LUNCHBOX. Now go to 51.

148

The children's quick discussion ended when they agreed that George's idea sounded the most sensible. That was, quite simply, to return to her cottage and ask Professor Hayling for directions to the lighthouse this time. The Professor and George's father weren't very pleased about yet another interruption but the Professor eventually told them that they should head in the direction of Sharprock Cliffs. He said that a footpath to Sharprock Cliffs passed exactly seventy metres from the little first-aid hut in Kirrin Bay. As soon as the children had reached the hut, they all started searching in their rucksacks for their measuring tapes.

Do you have a MEASURE in your RUCKSACK? If so, use it to measure the seventy metres from the first-aid hut – then follow the instruction there. (Remember to put the MEASURE CARD back in your RUCKSACK afterwards.) If you don't have one, you'll have to guess which instruction to follow.

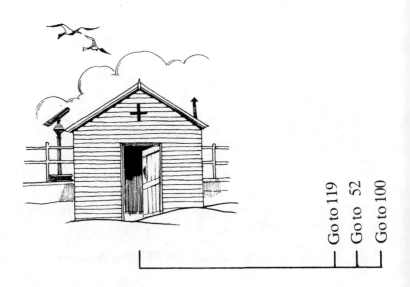

Go to 119
Go to 52
Go to 100

149

Just as the children were about to decode the instructions from the bird-watcher, however, the piece of paper was snatched from Dick's hand by a sudden gust of wind. 'Oh no, now we'll just have to guess the way!' Anne cried as the wind carried it higher and higher. They decided to head in the direction of an old copper mine in the distance. As they left the place where they had been sitting, however, they failed to notice that George's measuring tape was lying in the grass!

If you have it, remove the MEASURE CARD from your RUCKSACK. Now go to 200.

150

It took some time but, with the help of their codebooks, they finally cracked the code on the rock. The message read: *PATH INLAND IS A SHORT CUT TO WAILING LIGHTHOUSE. IT WILL REDUCE THE WALK BY NEARLY HALF*. 'That's exactly what we wanted to know,' remarked George excitedly, 'but I wonder who wrote the message.' Julian wondered too – and why the person had gone to all the trouble to put it in code. 'It's almost as if he didn't want too many people to know about the short cut,' he said thoughtfully. 'It sounds rather suspicious, doesn't it?' *Go to 191.*

151

As soon as the children had flashed a 'We're all right' Morse code message to the soldier, he waved goodbye to them and then disappeared behind the ridge again. They were just about to start moving again themselves when Timmy sniffed out a measuring tape in the grass. 'It must belong to one of the soldiers at the rifle range,' said Dick. 'They probably use them to make sure the targets are at exactly the right distance.'

If you don't already have it, put the MEASURE CARD into your RUCKSACK. Now go to 90.

They were all trying to feel for their torches in their rucksacks when there was a sudden shriek from the darkness ahead. The children quickly slung their rucksacks over their shoulders, running for all they were worth back towards the entrance. Once they were outside again, George, still trembling, asked: 'You don't think it could be the ghost of one of those drowned sailors, do you?' Their anxiety suddenly turned to laughter, though, as a gull flew out of the cave, landing at their feet. 'Of course, that's what the shriek was!' George chuckled and she was so relieved that she fed it a sandwich from her lunchbox before they re-entered the cave.

Take a PICNIC CARD from your LUNCHBOX. Now go to 27.

'These are obviously the caves here,' said Julian, pointing to the top corner of his map. He, George and Anne then started to fold their maps up again but Dick still kept his out. 'Are you sure you're right?' he asked, frowning heavily. The others immediately saw through this, though, and guessed that it was just a delaying tactic. 'You know full well we are, Dick,' Anne chuckled from behind. 'Come on – it's time you started moving again!' ***Go to 284.***

154

The Five didn't have to walk far from the youth hostel before they came to the sea again, finding themselves high up on the cliffs. Anne pointed to a strange formation in the rock just below them, asking Julian what it was. 'It's called a sea-arch,' he exclaimed. 'It's where the waves have eaten away at the rock so much that it forms a large hole right through.' He then suggested they look up the sea-arch on their maps so they would know how much further to go for the lighthouse.

Use your MAP to find out which square the sea-arch is in – then follow the instruction. If you don't have a MAP in your RUCKSACK, you'll have to guess which instruction to follow.

If you think E2	go to 8
If you think E3	go to 89
If you think E4	go to 173

155

The decoded message worked out as: *WE MUST MAKE SURE NO ONE ELSE SUSPECTS WHERE THE TREASURE IS OR WE'LL JUST HAVE TO HAND IT IN TO THE AUTHORITIES!* The Five all stared at each other in alarm when they learnt this. It very much sounded as if a gang of villains were on to the treasure! And the fact that the scrap of paper had been floating so far out suggested that this gang also, at some time, had crossed to the lighthouse. They could still be there even now! *Go to 185.*

Julian thought *he* had better go first since he was the eldest –
although this was one of those occasions when he rather wished he
wasn't! Having cautiously entered the lighthouse, he immediately
found himself at the foot of a spiral stairway. He led the way up the
crumbling stone steps, going round and round, until eventually he
reached a small circular room. 'This must have been where they
stored the oil,' he said, noticing several large rusty drums there.
They began to search the room – Dick suddenly discovering a
message chalked on to the wall. It read: *KEEP FOLLOWING
WALL ROUND FOR 50 METRES*.

**Use your MEASURE CARD to measure these fifty metres –
then follow the instruction there. If you don't have a MEASURE
in your RUCKSACK, you'll have to guess which instruction to
follow.**

Go to 111

Go to 291

Go to 13

They were just about to start decoding the message when a huge wave crashed right beside them, nearly sweeping them into the water! 'We'd better stand back a bit,' suggested Dick, but then they found that the message was too far away to read. Since it didn't seem worth the risk of going closer again, they decided they would just have to leave it. So they entered the lighthouse, immediately finding themselves at the foot of a stone stairway which they started to climb. The crumbling steps spiralled up and up, eventually reaching what looked like a small storeroom. The climb had been so exhausting, however, that they all decided to have a drink of their ginger beer before searching the room.

Take a PICNIC CARD from your LUNCHBOX. Now go to 12.

The Five had now searched every inch of the lighthouse, from top to bottom, but there was absolutely no sign of any treasure. 'Maybe the whole thing's just a made-up yarn after all,' said Dick, as they disappointedly made their way to the entrance again, to return to the shore. When they reached the door, however, they had a nasty shock. It was locked! 'Someone must have done it deliberately to keep us in!' exclaimed Dick in alarm. 'Whatever do we do now?' ***Go to 79.***

Julian said there wasn't time to look up their maps at the moment, though. They had to try and find a way out so they could inform the police about the gang! So he quickly led them back along the tunnel and towards the lighthouse again. 'We'll have another go at that locked door,' he told them on the way. 'We'll give it everything we've got this time!' *Go to 196.*

Finally arriving back at the lighthouse, they had another go at trying to force open the door. It was just as impossible as before, though, and so Julian quickly led the way up the stairs to the lamp-room. 'I've just had an idea,' he said eagerly. 'If we could manage to light the lamp, then it might well attract the police's attention. They'll probably wonder why the lighthouse has suddenly started flashing again!' So, the moment they reached the top of the lighthouse, Julian hurried over to the huge lamp, to see if he could figure out how it worked! *Go to 264.*

George was the first to find the stone pillar on her map, and she quickly showed it to the sergeant. 'Ah, we've come too far,' he said on briefly studying it. 'The stone bridge is back a bit!' So he began leading them in that direction, but they had still to spot the bridge when Timmy suddenly stopped. He had sniffed out a codebook on the rough ground. 'I wouldn't mind betting this was dropped by a member of the gang!' the sergeant remarked. 'Perhaps one of you children could put it in your rucksack so I can have a better look at it later? It might well be important evidence!'

If you don't already have it, put the CODEBOOK CARD into your RUCKSACK. Now go to 99.

162

Just as the children began to look for their torches, however, one of the gang glanced towards the boulders where they were hiding. 'Phew, for a moment I thought he had seen us!' said the sergeant, and he breathed a sigh of relief as the man looked away again. 'Anyway, I think perhaps we had better forget about that torch in case they notice the light.' They waited there in the darkness, therefore, George offering round the remainder of her sandwiches to help pass the time.

Take a PICNIC CARD from your LUNCHBOX. Now go to 134. (Remember: when there are no picnic cards left in your lunchbox the game is over, and you must start again.)

They were just about to agree that Dick's idea sounded best when
Professor Hayling came running after them. 'Oh, thank goodness
I've found you,' he panted. 'I've just remembered that I haven't told
you how to get to Wailing Lighthouse.' He added that being a
scientist made one very absent-minded! 'Anyway,' he said, 'the
quickest route is to cut across inland. Head for Whitedunes
campsite to begin with.' Before they could ask where Whitedunes
campsite was, however, the Professor had disappeared again! It was
a good job they had maps with them.

*Do you have a MAP in your RUCKSACK? If so, use it to find out
which square the campsite is in – then follow the instruction.
(Remember to put the MAP back in your RUCKSACK afterwards.) If you don't have a MAP, you'll have to guess which
instruction to follow.*

If you think A2   go to 16
If you think A3   go to 209
If you think B3   go to 277

164

They had still to decide who was to walk at the front along the
footpath when they spotted a man in a thick polo neck sweater
coming the other way. Written across the front of his sweater was
the word COASTGUARD. 'Hey! You children ought not to be
walking so close to the edge,' he shouted as he came nearer. 'Why
don't you take the other footpath that's slightly further in? It's much

safer. You'll find it eighty paces to your left.' The children followed the coastguard's advice, immediately starting to count out the eighty paces.

Do you have a MEASURE in your RUCKSACK? If so, use it to measure the eighty paces from the coastguard – then follow the instruction there. If you don't have one, you'll have to guess which instruction to follow.

Go to 54

Go to 2

Go to 236

165

When they had found the statue on their maps, George had another suggestion. 'I'm absolutely starving,' she said. 'Before we take the path towards Wailing Lighthouse, let's have some of our picnic.' And she immediately plonked herself on to the ground so there could be no argument about it!

Take a PICNIC CARD from your LUNCHBOX. Now go to 191.

'Oh, I don't think there's anything to worry about after all,' Dick said suddenly. 'Those bangs are just from an army shooting range, I'm sure of it. They often have them in deserted areas like this!' His theory seemed to be confirmed by Julian's discovery, a little further along, of a small card with black circles on it. 'Look, it's a miniature target,' he said. 'One of the soldiers must have dropped it on his way back from the shooting range.' He was just about to put the paper target in his pocket as a souvenir when he noticed a coded message scribbled across the top!

Use your CODEBOOK CARD to find out what the message on the target said by decoding the instruction below. If you don't have a CODEBOOK in your RUCKSACK, go to 40 instead.

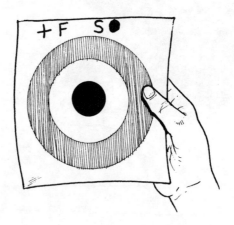

To do the measuring, of course, it was necessary for one person to stay behind at the sign with one end of the tape. They decided that this person should be Dick; the others taking the spool. As they disappeared into the darkness, though, Dick became rather nervous and couldn't help edging after them a bit. In fact, he moved so far forward that the others reached the pothole sooner than they were expecting and Julian stepped right into it! He fell across the cave's hard floor, his rucksack slipping from his shoulders. Fortunately, Julian wasn't hurt at all – but no one noticed that his map had dropped out!

If you have it, remove the MAP from your RUCKSACK. Now go to 284.

168

They finally decoded the message on the youth hostel flagpole as: *WAILING LIGHTHOUSE CAN BE SEEN AFTER ANOTHER HALF MILE.* 'Great!' said Julian as they put their codebooks away again. 'That's exactly what we wanted to know!' Eagerly continuing on their way, however, they couldn't help thinking that there was something rather suspicious about the coded message being there. 'In fact there was something rather suspicious about that unfriendly man at the hostel as well,' Dick remarked. 'Do you think he was just the old warden still looking after the place? Or do you think he had a more sinister reason for being there?' *Go to 42.*

169

They took so long looking for their codebooks in their rucksacks that, by the time they had found them, the oil drum was gone. A large wave had come in and washed it out to sea! 'If we wait, perhaps another wave will bring it back in again,' said Dick but the drum only drifted further and further out. They were all so disappointed at losing what might have been a very important message that they sat down for a while, and had a drink from their bottles of ginger beer. Feeling much better after that, they prepared to enter the cave again!

Take a PICNIC CARD from your LUNCHBOX. Now go to 27.

170

It was *George* who reached Jeremiah Boogle's cottage first, arriving a fraction before the others. They were about to knock on the ramshackle door when they spotted a note pinned to it. Scrawled in a semi-literate hand was the message: *I GON TO HAVE A SMOKE OF ME PIPE. IF ANY FOLK BE WANTING ME, WALK 120 PACES TOWARDS LOBSTER POTS.* They looked around for some lobster pots, suddenly spotting a whole heap of them much further along the bay. Seconds later, they were counting out the paces towards them!

Use your MEASURE CARD to measure the 120 paces from the

*cottage door – then follow the instruction there. If you don't have a **MEASURE** in your **RUCKSACK**, you'll have to guess which instruction to follow.*

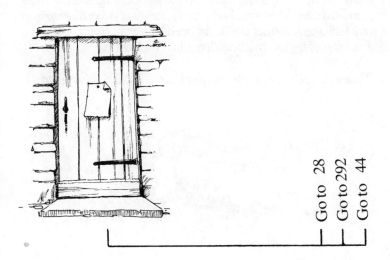

Go to 28
Go to 292
Go to 44

171

The children were just opening their codebooks when a large wave crashed against their rowing-boat, drenching the inside. 'Oh no,' Anne tutted, 'it's washed off the message!' A lot of the water had also splashed in George's face, leaving a horrible salty taste in her mouth. She took a large gulp of her ginger beer to get rid of it!

*Take a **PICNIC CARD** from your **LUNCHBOX**. Now go to 185.*

No sooner had Anne produced her measuring tape, however, than they immediately came up against a problem. No one was prepared to stay behind to hold the tape's end while the others all went off with the spool! 'Well, we'll just have to guess at the forty metres,' said Julian eventually, 'and make sure we keep our eyes open!' So they all carefully continued up the steps. Dick was just about to turn round to say that the forty-metre mark should be coming up soon when he stumbled over a trip-wire. Fortunately, the others were there to stop him falling any further but he dropped his lunchbox in the tumble and most of his sandwiches fell out into the dust!

Take a PICNIC CARD from your LUNCHBOX. Now go to 94.

As the children tried to open their maps to look up the sea-arch, though, Timmy leapt around them excitedly. 'Stop it, Timmy,' Dick ordered crossly. 'How can I find out where we are when you're jumping all over me!' Anne suddenly realised the reason for Timmy's excitement, however. His paw kept pointing to something to their left – and that something was the lighthouse! It stood grey and silent on its little rocky island, just out to sea. 'Oh, well spotted, Timmy!' Dick cheered, giving him a hug. 'And since I was so horrible to you, you can have one of my sandwiches!'

Take a PICNIC CARD from your LUNCHBOX. Now go to 25.
(Remember: when there are no picnic cards left in your lunchbox, the game is over and you must start again.)

Dick led the way down the shaft, being very careful not to slip from the iron rungs. It grew darker and darker as he descended and he decided he'd better use his torch. Unfortunately, it was still in his rucksack on his back and, since he couldn't reach it himself, he asked Julian, who was coming down just behind him, to get it out. 'I'll stop a minute while you reach inside,' he called up.

Use your TORCH CARD to help light up the shaft for Dick by placing exactly over the shape below – then follow the instruction. If you don't have a TORCH in your RUCKSACK, go to 14 instead.

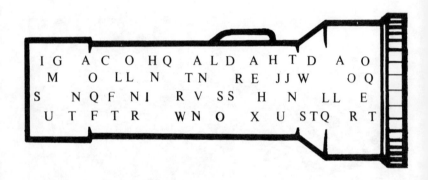

```
I G    A  C  O  HQ    A L D    A  H T D    A   O
   M     O  LL  N    TN    R E   J J W       O Q
S    N Q F  N I    R V  SS   H   N     L L     E
  U  T  F  T  R      WN  O    X   U  STQ    R T
```

The children were just about to open their maps to look up the ship's bell when Jeremiah Boogle appeared! He explained to them that the bell was in memory of all the sailors who had drowned in these parts, and he thought it only right that someone should look after it. 'Anyway, why you be wanting to call on ol' Jeremiah?' he asked, puffing at his pipe. Julian said that they would like to borrow his rowing-boat, offering him a pound for it. 'Cert'nly you can borrow it,' Jeremiah told him. 'But a pound ain't necessary! I'll just settle for a bite to eat from your lunchbox there!'

Take a PICNIC CARD from your LUNCHBOX. Now go to 10.

Anne was the first to find her codebook, and she immediately handed it to Julian. Thanking her, he started to decode the message on the candle before the flame melted some of it away. 'Just did it in time,' he exclaimed, after flicking through the book's pages. 'It said that the candle was the property of the lighthouse keeper. That means he must have come to this tunnel sometimes! I wonder why.' *Go to 207.*

All telling George how brilliant her idea was, they immediately fished out their torches and held them up against the glass. They then started to flash them at regular intervals towards the shore. 'The sky seems to be growing darker by the second,' Dick observed joyfully. 'So our torches should soon be clear as anything!' *Go to 117.*

'There are the steps!' Anne suddenly cried, pointing into the darkness. 'Can you see? – just over there!' The police boat immediately came ashore and they were all soon climbing these steps. 'The stone bridge should be in *that* direction!' the sergeant remarked when they had at last reached the top and he hurriedly led the way inland. After a while, though, he suddenly stopped in great confusion, saying they must have made a wrong turn somewhere in the dark. Spotting an ancient stone pillar nearby, he asked the children to look it up on their maps so that they would know where they were.

Use your MAP to find out which square the ancient stone pillar is in – then follow the instruction. If you don't have a MAP in your RUCKSACK, you'll have to guess which instruction to follow.

If you think A2	go to 161
If you think B2	go to 246
If you think B1	go to 276

179

Measuring the eighty metres from the water-tap, The Five soon found the footpath which the man had described. They were just about to follow it when the man hurried across after them. 'I've just thought of something,' he panted, waving a small book at them. 'If you're going to Wailing Lighthouse, you'll probably need this codebook. A lot of the signposts on the way are in a special code, dating back to the time when wreckers lived in the area.'

If you don't already have it, put the CODEBOOK CARD into your RUCKSACK. Now go to 53.

Finally, having counted out the 160 paces towards the tenth hole, they found that they had reached flag number nine! 'Whatever this thing is that can help must be down in the hole,' Julian said, crouching down to have a look. But, other than the end of the flagpole, the hole was completely empty. 'Someone must have been and taken it already,' Julian remarked as he stood up again. 'I wonder what on earth it was?' To make up for their disappointment, George suggested they all have a quick drink of ginger beer before continuing.

Take a PICNIC CARD from your LUNCHBOX. Now go to 191.

181

'Look – here's the shooting range!' Julian told the others as he located it on his map. 'Well I never – Timmy was absolutely right about it!' George said of course Timmy was right about it – he was the cleverest dog there was! 'And the bravest!' she added, just for good measure. ***Go to 41.***

Dick reached the youth hostel first, arriving just ahead of Julian and Timmy. 'Gosh, isn't it dark!' he exclaimed as he led the way in. 'I don't think we're going to find anyone to ask about Wailing Lighthouse after all. This place obviously hasn't been used for years!' They had just decided to leave again when Julian suddenly had an idea. 'Youth hostels usually have lots of information about the local area pinned to a notice-board,' he said. 'Maybe there's something still there to show how far it is to the lighthouse!' They were only likely to find this notice-board, though, with the help of their torches.

Use your TORCH CARD to light up the inside of the youth hostel by placing exactly over the shape below – then follow the instruction. If you don't have a TORCH in your RUCKSACK, go to 278 instead.

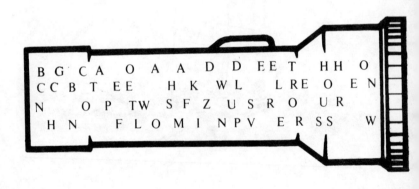

'That's better!' said Dick, flashing his torch around the cave's damp walls. 'No sign of any treasure yet, though!' Or was there? For, just as he pointed his torch down at the rocky floor in front of them, something reflected the torch's beam. He hurried up to it to investigate. It unfortunately wasn't a piece of priceless jewellery like he had hoped for but just the shiny cover of a map of the area. Still, the map was a lot more detailed than any of theirs and so he decided to pop it in his rucksack.

If you don't already have it, put the MAP into your RUCK-SACK. Now go to 27.

184

'There seems to be nothing here but a pile of old fishing nets!' said Anne when they had measured the 110 paces from Jeremiah Boogle's cottage. They were just beginning to think that the old man had tricked them out of fifty pence when Timmy started to tug the top fishing net off. Then he tugged at the second and the third, finally revealing something wooden underneath. 'Why, Jeremiah didn't trick us after all!' George exclaimed as she gave her dog a proud pat. 'Look – *here's* the rowing-boat!' *Go to 10.*

185

Eventually they reached the little rocky island on which the lighthouse stood, rowing the boat round to a place where it seemed safe to land. As they pulled the boat ashore, they all stared at the lighthouse soaring high above them, silent and mysterious. 'Gosh, it looks even eerier close to!' Dick gulped as they walked tentatively round its base, looking for the door. When they found it, they weren't sure whether they wanted it to be unlocked or not! But it *was* unlocked, and, as they pushed it open, it made a horrible creaking sound. They then nervously discussed who was going to step through first.

Throw *THE FAMOUS FIVE DICE* to decide.

JULIAN thrown	go to 223
DICK thrown	go to 45
GEORGE thrown	go to 257
ANNE thrown	go to 204
TIMMY thrown	go to 272
MYSTERY thrown	go to 241

186

'Where *are* these steps?' Julian asked bewilderedly after they had measured the ninety metres from the old signpost. They just couldn't understand it. They were positive they hadn't made any mistake in their measuring, but there wasn't a step to be seen! 'I know what might have happened!' said Dick suddenly. 'You remember the signpost was a bit loose? Well, perhaps it's been twisted round by the strong wind up here and is pointing the wrong way.' So they all returned to the signpost, and measured ninety metres in the other direction. Somehow they felt they were going to be more lucky this time! *Go to 7.*

Dick volunteered to stay there with the end of the measuring tape while the others continued on down with the spool. He had to wait for a good five minutes but then he suddenly heard a cry of 'We've reached it!' from below. He hurried down to join the others, asking whether there was anything there. 'Well, it's not the treasure like we'd hoped,' replied Julian. 'But there was this codebook. It was resting on a little ledge, exactly the distance down the message said!'

If you don't already have it, put the CODEBOOK CARD into your RUCKSACK. Now go to 216.

Before they could stop him, Timmy suddenly bounded off in the direction of the bird-watcher! 'How can *he* possibly ask the way to Wailing Lighthouse?' the others all laughed. 'The bird-watcher won't know what he's barking about!' The children were right because as soon as Timmy reached the bird-watcher, the man shouted at him to go away. 'Oh dear, it looks as if his barking has frightened the birds and made him angry,' George remarked. As Timmy sheepishly returned, Dick noticed some sort of coded message painted on a nearby rock. 'Quick, let's get out our codebooks,' he urged them excitedly. 'Maybe *this* has something to do with the way to Wailing Lighthouse!'

Do you have a CODEBOOK in your RUCKSACK? If so, use it

to find out what the coded message said by decoding the instruction below. If you don't have one, go to 270 instead.

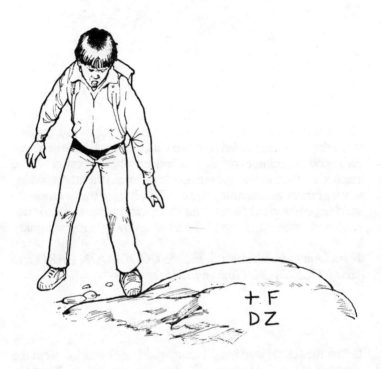

+ F
D Z

Being the first to find his torch, Dick immediately pointed it into the tunnel. 'Ah, that's much better!' he exclaimed as the first twenty metres or so suddenly lit up. 'OK, Timmy, you can lead the way now!' They hadn't walked very far along the tunnel when they heard a faint swirling noise from above. It sounded like the sea! Julian must have been right, then – the tunnel did run beneath it!
Go to 207.

'It works out as: *WE'LL BE WAITING AT THE STONE BRIDGE,*' Julian said bewilderedly when he had decoded the message on the sheet. 'I wonder who it was left for – and why the gang made it so big.' The rest of The Five were equally puzzled by it but the sergeant gave a chuckle, telling them to think why it might be spread out on the ground. 'Of course!' exclaimed Dick, suddenly realising. 'It's so it can be seen from the air. This is obviously a message to the plane that's going to collect them!' *Go to 51.*

'I wonder how much further,' Dick said some time later, as the land between them and the lighthouse just seemed to stretch on and on. 'It surely can't be more than another mile or so.' Just at that moment there was a series of deafening bangs from behind the ridge to their right. 'Gosh, what's that!' exclaimed George in terror. 'It sounds like someone's shooting!' The bangs came again and they all tried to work out what they might be.

Throw the FAMOUS FIVE DICE to decide who realises first.

JULIAN thrown	go to 249
DICK thrown	go to 166
GEORGE thrown	go to 24
ANNE thrown	go to 202
TIMMY thrown	go to 219
MYSTERY thrown	go to 88

The flag waved about so much in the wind, however, that decoding the message on it proved impossible. The letters and symbols just wouldn't stay still long enough! 'Oh, we might as well give up,' said Julian, putting his codebook away again. 'We'll be here all day otherwise!' Before they left the youth hostel and continued on their way, they all decided to have a quick sandwich or two from their lunchboxes. They were feeling quite hungry!

Take a PICNIC CARD from your LUNCHBOX. Now go to 42.

George finally agreed to enter the lighthouse first and she led the way into the musty interior. Finding herself at the foot of a spiral staircase, she cautiously started to climb it. The crumbling stone steps went round and round until eventually they reached a small circular room. 'It must have been the keeper's living-quarters,' said Julian, spotting a rusty old bed there. 'Hey, what's this on the floor? It looks like an old knuckleduster!' Turning the nasty-looking object over in his hand, he noticed some sort of coded message inscribed on it.

Use your CODEBOOK CARD to find out what the message said by decoding the instruction below. If you don't have one, go to 240 instead.

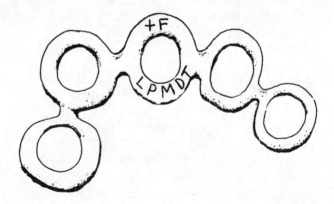

Finally managing to find Dick's torch in his rucksack, Julian switched it on for him and passed it down. 'It would have made it a lot easier if you'd already had your torch out!' he told him with a chuckle. Dick totally agreed, not being able to understand why he didn't *think* before entering the shaft. It should have been quite obvious that his torch was going to be needed! *Go to 31.*

They were just about to start measuring when the tunnel roof suddenly began to drip. 'Oh, it's leaking!' Anne cried. 'Let's just leave the measuring and hurry out of here!' Julian tried all he could to reassure her, saying that it had probably been doing that for years. Seeing how anxious she still was, however, he did as she asked and hurriedly started moving again. He went a bit *too* fast, though, because some distance further on he suddenly tripped and broke his ginger beer bottle!

Take a PICNIC CARD from your LUNCHBOX. Now go to 207.

They finally reached the lighthouse again but, however hard they tried, the door proved just as impossible to open as before. 'What do we do now?' Dick asked despondently. Suddenly George had an idea! 'Follow me!' she cried – and she hurriedly led them up the spiral steps to the lamp-room at the top. 'We can flash our torches through the glass as a signal,' she explained, panting. 'They should be seen for miles once it gets dark. And, look, the daylight's beginning to fade already!'

*Use your **TORCH CARD** to flash this signal by placing exactly over the shape below – then follow the instruction. If you don't have a **TORCH** in your **RUCKSACK**, go to 32 instead.*

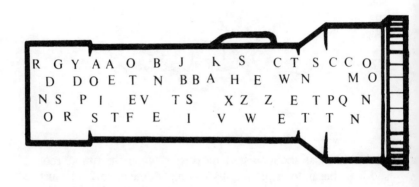

197
As soon as the children had switched on their torches, the sergeant led the way up the steps. During their climb, Dick anxiously asked Julian whether he thought they might be too late to stop the gang by now. 'Well, we haven't seen or heard a plane fly over yet,' Julian replied optimistically, 'so let's hope there's still a bit of time!' ***Go to 217.***

198
'Just as I thought – this belongs to one of the gang!' the sergeant exclaimed when he had helped Anne decode the message on the banknote. 'It works out as *PLANE WILL BE ARRIVING TO*

COLLECT US AT MIDNIGHT. One of the gang members is obviously so stupid that he had to write it down to remember!' As they continued towards the top of the steps, Julian asked the sergeant why the banknote was a French one. 'Well, that plane is probably taking them to France,' the sergeant replied. ***Go to 51.***

199

'It's a lot windier than it was down at the bay,' Anne remarked as the footpath they followed climbed higher and higher. The path soon started to run perilously close to the edge as well and so Julian suggested they walk single file for a while until it became safer again. 'Right, who's going to walk at the front?' he asked.

Throw the FAMOUS FIVE DICE to decide who it's to be.

JULIAN thrown	go to 299
DICK thrown	go to 85
GEORGE thrown	go to 102
ANNE thrown	go to 37
TIMMY thrown	go to 248
MYSTERY thrown	go to 164

200

The Five had walked across the rough ground for another mile or so when they came to a deserted golf course. They were just passing the seventh hole when Timmy started sniffing at the bottom of the flagpost. He then clawed at the hole. 'Timmy DON'T, or you'll get your paw stuck!' George shouted at him but he continued to dig. Eventually, George had to drag him away from the hole but as she did so she noticed there was an old piece of cloth at the bottom. Pulling it out, she saw that there was a message embroidered on it. It read: *ABE – TO HELP YOU LOOK FOR TREASURE IN THE CAVES, WALK 160 PACES TOWARDS HOLE 10.* As you can guess, it wasn't long before The Five began to count the 160 paces!

Do you have a MEASURE in your RUCKSACK? If so, use it to measure the 160 paces from the flag at the seventh hole – then follow the instruction there. If you don't have one, you'll have to guess which instruction to follow.

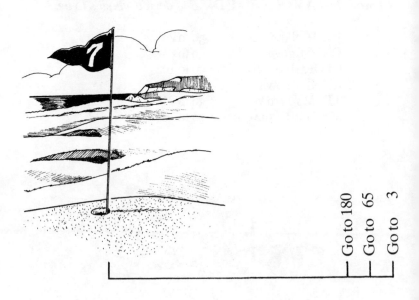

Go to 180
Go to 65
Go to 3

201

The children were still searching for their maps in their rucksacks, taking everything out, when there was another series of bangs from behind the ridge. Timmy was convinced the bangs signified trouble and suddenly dashed off towards the ridge to investigate! George began to chase after him, ordering him to come back, but it was only when Timmy finally reached the ridge and saw the firing range for himself that he did so. '*Now* are you satisfied, Timmy?' George demanded rather crossly. She would have been even more cross if she had known that he had caused her to leave her codebook on the ground!

If you have it, remove the CODEBOOK CARD from your RUCKSACK. Now go to 90.

202

'I've got it!' exclaimed Anne suddenly. 'You're right, George, those bangs *are* someone shooting. They're from an army firing range – where they practise!' The others all clapped Anne on the back, convinced that she was correct. Their minds at rest, they started walking again but Julian made them stop suddenly, just as they were passing a slab of rock which stuck upright in the ground. On it someone had chalked the words: *FOR SECRET CODEBOOK, WALK 70 METRES TOWARDS FIRING RANGE.* The children immediately went to their rucksacks for their measuring tapes!

Use your MEASURE CARD to measure the seventy metres from the upright stone – then follow the instruction there. If you

don't have a MEASURE in your RUCKSACK, you'll have to guess which instruction to follow.

Go to 139

Go to 73

Go to 106

203

They were just starting to decode the message on the youth hostel flagpole when the man appeared at the door once more. 'I thought I told you lot to be off!' he shouted at them. 'Get going or I'll call the police!' So The Five had no choice but to leave the coded message, continuing on their way. 'What a nasty man that warden was,' Julian remarked as he passed round his ginger beer. 'In fact, I wonder if he was a warden at all, being up to no good there!'

Take a PICNIC CARD from your LUNCHBOX. Now go to 42.

204

Anne thought that standing there talking about it was only making their nerves a lot worse and so, much to the other's surprise, *she* offered to enter the lighthouse first. 'Make sure you all stay close behind, though,' she said as she made her way through the half-darkness to the bottom of a spiral staircase. It became harder and harder to see as she led them up the stone stairs and she brought them to a halt for a moment, suggesting they switch on one of their torches.

Use your TORCH CARD to light the stairway up by placing exactly over the shape below – then follow the instruction. If you don't have a TORCH in your RUCKSACK, go to 29 instead.

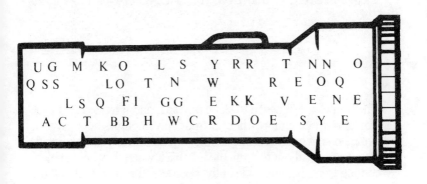

```
U G  M  K O    L S    Y R R     T  N N     O
Q S S      L O   T  N     W         R  E  O Q
     L S Q  FI   G G     E  K K    V   E  N  E
  A C T   B B  H  W C R   D O E     S Y    E
```

205

'I wonder what that's all about?' asked Julian when he had decoded the message on the rock. It worked out as: *TRICK LIGHT-HOUSE KEEPER BY SAYING YOU'VE COME WITH SUPPLIES*. Then he suddenly realised. It must have been carved there all those years back by that evil gang who doused the light! 'That was obviously how they deceived the keeper into letting them in,' he explained as they now cautiously entered the lighthouse themselves. They immediately met a spiral staircase and started to climb it, eventually reaching a small dark room. 'It looks like it was once the storeroom,' said Dick as they searched around. *Go to 12.*

So that no one would have to stop there holding the end of the measuring tape, George had the clever idea of tying it to a rung. They then all continued down the shaft, unwinding the tape's spool as they descended. Suddenly, though, the end George thought she had tied came slithering down after them, dropping on to Anne's face. It gave her such a shock that she let go of her lunchbox! 'You idiot, George,' Dick told her crossly. 'Now, not only has Anne lost her entire picnic but we won't know what that message wanted us to find!'

Take a PICNIC CARD from your LUNCHBOX. Now go to 216.

The tunnel at last began to slope upwards and it looked as if they would soon be coming to the end. Suddenly, though, they arrived at a huge pile of boulders, impossible to pass! Bitterly disappointed, they were just about to go all the way back when they heard voices coming from the other side of the boulders. 'I reckon that's all the treasure found now, then, lads,' one of them said. 'Let's shift it up to the stone bridge ready for the plane to collect us tonight!' The children all stared at each other in bewilderment, wondering what to make of this. Suddenly, Julian snapped his fingers, certain that he had the explanation! *Go to 17.*

'Here it is!' said Anne, who was the first to find the bird reserve on her map. She pointed it out to the sergeant who quickly scanned it for the stone bridge. 'Ah, there it is,' he remarked thoughtfully. 'That means we want to head due north from here!' He pointed to his right. 'It should be over that way,' he added, breaking into another run. 'Come on, everybody!' *Go to 99.*

'Look, it's only about half a mile away,' Julian said, when they had found the campsite on their maps. So they immediately began walking towards it, following a rough road which started at the back of Kirrin Bay. 'This must be it,' exclaimed Dick when they had reached a dozen or so tents in an area of grassland. As they were wandering through the campsite, Anne suddenly spotted a torch lying on the ground!

If you don't already have it, put the TORCH CARD into your RUCKSACK. Now go to 53.

'Since it's your idea, Anne,' laughed the others, 'maybe *you* should be the one to go and ask the bird-watcher!' The bird-watcher told her that he had never heard of Wailing Lighthouse but pointed out an old stone tower some distance ahead. 'Why don't you try climbing that?' he suggested kindly. 'You might get a glimpse of your lighthouse from the top!' Anne immediately ran back to the others with this idea and it wasn't long before they were on the balcony of the tower. They *could* just see the lighthouse! 'Let's look up this tower on our maps as well,' suggested George. 'Then we'll know exactly where we are!'

Do you have a MAP in your RUCKSACK? If so, use it to find out which square the old stone tower is in – then follow the instruction. If you don't have one, you'll have to guess which instruction to follow.

If you think C2	go to 39
If you think B3	go to 136
If you think C3	go to 265

211

The path twisted and turned to the very bottom of the cliffs, finally reaching a narrow bay. They were surprised to find a couple of tiny cottages there. 'They must belong to fishermen,' said Julian as they passed them on their way to the furthest end of the bay. It was at the very end, where the sea seemed at its wildest, that the caves were! 'Gosh, they're much bigger than they looked from the cliff-top,' Dick remarked as they slowly approached, '– and scarier!' They were at last standing at the mouth of one of the caves and they hesitated for a moment, wondering who was going to enter first!

Throw the FAMOUS FIVE DICE to decide who it's going to be.

JULIAN thrown	go to 230
DICK thrown	go to 5
GEORGE thrown	go to 123
ANNE thrown	go to 279
TIMMY thrown	go to 262
MYSTERY thrown	go to 295

Not surprisingly, it was Timmy who won the race to the youth hostel! They now prepared to enter it but, when they tried the door, they found that it was well and truly locked. 'It looks as if it's no longer in use,' said Julian. 'We might as well continue on our way.' Just as they were about to start walking again, however, Dick noticed a coded message embroidered across the bottom of the youth hostel flag. They all immediately dived for their codebooks!

Use your CODEBOOK CARD to find out what the message said by decoding the instruction below. If you don't have a CODEBOOK in your RUCKSACK, go to 192 instead.

'Oh, it's only a short distance away!' George told the others, as she was the first to find the ship's bell on her map. 'We shouldn't have to wait too long for him!' In fact, Jeremiah Boogle came walking along the bay only a few minutes later, soon reaching them. When they asked if they could borrow his boat, he was perfectly happy to oblige, taking them round to an upturned skiff at the back of the cottage. When he turned it the right way up for them, he was surprised to find an old measuring tape underneath!

If you don't already have it, put the MEASURE CARD into your RUCKSACK. Now go to 10.

214

Finally reaching the first of the caves, The Five cautiously made their way inside. 'Ooh, isn't it scary,' said George as their footsteps echoed in the darkness. 'I hope we don't take too long finding the treasure!' After a good half hour of feeling all along the damp walls, however, they still hadn't discovered a thing. As they turned to work their way back to the entrance again, a shadowy figure suddenly appeared in front of them! 'Don't go alarming yerselves!' it chuckled as Anne gave a frightened shriek. 'I ain't be meaning yer no 'arm. Me name's Ebenezer.' ***Go to 110.***

Dick told Anne that he could only reach down into her rucksack by taking one hand off the rungs, however, and that would make him unsafe. 'Oh, yes, I forgot about that,' Anne apologised from below. 'We'll just have to leave this coded message, then, and hope it's not too important!' She continued her climb down the rungs but she hadn't descended much further when her foot suddenly slipped. Fortunately, she just managed to stop herself from falling but her lunchbox jerked out of the top of her rucksack and disappeared into the darkness below!

Take a PICNIC CARD from your LUNCHBOX. Now go to 31.

The children at last reached the bottom of the shaft, discovering a long tunnel leading off from it! 'It must run under the sea!' exclaimed Julian. 'There's nowhere else it can go. And, with any luck, it might lead all the way back to the shore!' So they decided to risk following the tunnel. It was so narrow, however, that there was only room to walk along it in single file.

Throw THE FAMOUS FIVE DICE to decide who is to go first along the tunnel.

JULIAN thrown	go to 80
DICK thrown	go to 244
GEORGE thrown	go to 296
ANNE thrown	go to 115
TIMMY thrown	go to 64
MYSTERY thrown	go to 130

At last they reached the top of the steps and found themselves standing on the cliff-tops. 'Now, you say this gang is to be picked up by their plane at the stone bridge?' the sergeant checked with the children quickly. 'Perhaps one of you could take your map out so I can work out which direction the bridge is?'

Use your MAP to find out which square the stone bridge is in – then follow the instruction. If you don't have a MAP in your RUCKSACK, you'll have to guess which instruction to follow.

If you think B2   go to 19
If you think C1   go to 96
If you think B1   go to 256

'Look – here it is!' exclaimed Anne, the first to find Kirrin Bay on her map. As soon as they had worked out the lighthouse's direction from the bay they all put their maps away again and started walking. 'Of course, you know who that island belongs to?' George bragged as Julian led the way. The others knew full well that it belonged to *George* – it had been in her family for generations and was given to her by her mother – but they deliberately didn't answer! ***Go to 199.***

The first to realise the meaning of the bangs was *Timmy*, pointing his paw to a red flag at one end of the ridge. 'Now, why are you drawing our attention to that, Timmy?' George asked but then she remembered where she had seen a flag like that before. 'Of course – it was at an army shooting range on a moor Timmy and I once went to!' she exclaimed. As she gave her dog a proud hug, the others decided to look up the army shooting range on their maps. It would show them roughly where they were!

Use your MAP to find out which square the shooting range is in – then follow the instruction. If you don't have a MAP in your RUCKSACK, you'll have to guess which instruction to follow.

If you think D2	go to 138
If you think D3	go to 181
If you think D4	go to 41

They were still feeling around in their rucksacks for their torches, when it was George's turn to fall over! 'You can forget about your torches, everybody,' she said bad-temperedly as she picked herself up again. 'I've *found* Dick's ginger beer bottle. It was right under my feet!' She was so cross with Dick for making her slip on his bottle that she refused to give it back until she had taken a long drink from 'it! They now left the hostel and continued on their way.

Take a *PICNIC CARD* from your *LUNCHBOX*. Now go to 154.

Shining their torches over the youth hostel's dark, dusty walls, they eventually found a notice-board. There were still some maps and information sheets pinned to it as well! 'Ah, this is what we wanted!' said Julian, pointing to a rough map in the middle. 'Look – it shows that the bay opposite Wailing Lighthouse is about another half mile's walk. That means we should reach it in a quarter of an hour!' *Go to 154.*

'It looks like Jeremiah has just tricked us out of fifty pence,' Julian remarked crossly when they had walked the 110 paces along the bay. 'Look – there's nothing here but a great big pile of lobster pots!' When they had returned to Jeremiah's cottage, however, the old man insisted that it wasn't a trick and accompanied them *back* to the lobster pots. 'See – there me boat is,' he told them, lifting some of the pots off. 'It's hidden underneath!' Julian felt so guilty about mistrusting Jeremiah that he gave him his largest slice of cake!

Take a PICNIC CARD from your LUNCHBOX. Now go to 10.

Julian thought they would be discussing it all day if someone didn't make a move and so *he* entered the lighthouse first. He immediately found himself at the bottom of a spiral stairway and led the way up the crumbling steps. They hadn't gone far, however, when Dick noticed a message on the wall. It read: *WHEN SHIP ON ROCKS, FLASH SIGNAL TO OTHERS AT OLD MILL.* 'This must have been written by someone from that evil gang all those years ago,' he said excitedly. 'The signal was probably to tell

the gang members on land to come and sort through the wreckage!'
He suggested they look up the old mill on their maps, just out of
interest.

*Use your MAP to find out which square the old mill is in – then
follow the instruction.*

If you think B2	go to 94
If you think B1	go to 112
If you think A1	go to 78

224

Quickly flicking through his codebook, Julian worked out the
coded inscription on the knuckleduster as: *THIS IS THE
PROPERTY OF ONE-EAR BILL*. When the others asked who
he thought One-Ear Bill was, Julian said that he must have been one
of that evil gang who doused the lighthouse's lamp. 'And this
horrible thing here,' he added, slipping the knuckleduster over his
fingers to show how it was worn, 'was probably what he used to
overpower the keeper!' *Go to 62.*

225

The police motor-boat was soon nearing the shore, the cliffs
towering above. 'There's a series of steps somewhere which leads to
the top,' the sergeant said as he ordered his pilot to chug along the

dark coastline. 'We'll land the boat there!' So The Five all peered out at the cliffs, searching for these steps.

Throw THE FAMOUS FIVE DICE to decide who is to spot them first.

JULIAN thrown	go to 133
DICK thrown	go to 83
GEORGE thrown	go to 146
ANNE thrown	go to 178
TIMMY thrown	go to 18
MYSTERY thrown	go to 67

226

While Julian was taking out his codebook, George came over to join him, asking what he had found. She became so excited when he told her it was a coded message that she accidentally gave the bell a nudge, knocking all the dust off. So, when Julian turned back to look at the message, it was gone! George quickly gave him a piece of cake from her lunchbox before he called her any names!

Take a PICNIC CARD from your LUNCHBOX. Now go to 158. (Remember: when there are no picnic cards left in your lunchbox the game is over, and you must start again.)

'All right, Timmy – we'll choose your idea!' the children laughed as George's dog insistently pointed his paw at a small campsite just back from Kirrin Bay. His idea was obviously to ask one of the campers the way. So they all followed Timmy over to the campsite, walking up to a man who was tightening the ropes on his tent. 'Wailing Lighthouse?' The man considered for a moment, 'Well, the quickest way is probably to take the small footpath which passes eighty metres from that water-tap over there.' The Five hurried across to the water-tap, taking out their measuring tapes on the way.

Do you have a MEASURE in your RUCKSACK? If so, use it to measure the eighty metres from the water-tap – then follow the instruction there. (Remember to put the MEASURE CARD back in your RUCKSACK afterwards.) If you don't have one, you'll have to guess which instruction to follow.

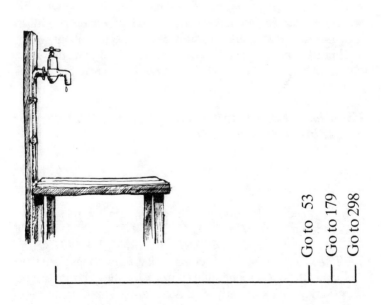

Go to 53

Go to 179

Go to 298

228

'It's a plastic measuring tape,' Julian told the others as he shone Anne's torch into the hole. 'Someone must have dropped it as they were walking along the path!' The torch not only lit up what the object was but it showed that the hole wasn't quite as deep as Julian had thought. In fact, the measuring tape was just about within reaching distance and, since a spare one might well prove useful, he put in his hand. 'Got it!' he exclaimed, and he transferred it to his rucksack.

If you don't already have it, put the TORCH CARD into your RUCKSACK. Now go to 137.

229

Using his codebook to decode the writing on the rock, Julian worked it out as: *WAILING LIGHTHOUSE – FOR RIGHT DIRECTION, HEAD TOWARDS CHIMNEY IN THE DISTANCE.* He wondered what chimney it was referring to but then he spotted the top of a long, thin chimney poking out from behind the next ridge. It looked as if it was part of an old copper mine. Now he knew which direction to go, he ran back to tell the others! *Go to 200.*

Since no one else seemed keen to do so, it was eventually Julian who entered the cave first. He hadn't led them far into its interior, however, when he noticed a sign fixed to the rocky wall. It read: *BEWARE HIDDEN POTHOLE 30 METRES FURTHER IN*. He told them all to take out their measuring tapes!

Use your MEASURE CARD to measure the thirty metres from the sign – then follow the instruction there. If you don't have a MEASURE in your RUCKSACK, you'll have to guess which instruction to follow.

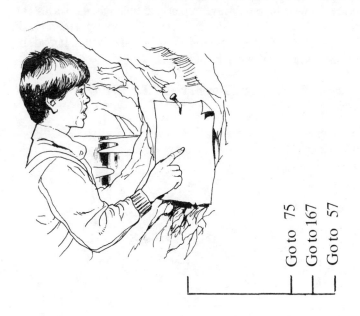

Go to 75

Go to 167

Go to 57

'This must be it!' exclaimed Dick when, having counted the 140 paces from the youth hostel flagpole, they reached a shallow track in the ground. As they followed this path, Anne asked if *they* could stay in a youth hostel one day. The others all thought it a good idea and said they'd consider it for their very next holiday! *Go to 154.*

'Who are you?' Julian demanded as their torches shone upon a rather ugly, unshaven face. They were relieved to see that it was at least a human face! 'Oh, no need for worrying yerselves,' the stranger reassured them with a toothy grin. 'I do yer no harm. I goes by the name of Ebenezer!' *Go to 110.*

Their maps were getting such a drenching from the amount of spray coming into the boat, however, that they had to put them away again before they had a chance to find Bell Rocks. 'Well, I'm sure it's nowhere near here anyway,' remarked Julian as the waves continued to beat at the boat's side. So that the choppy sea didn't make her seasick, George munched on one of her sandwiches. It made her queasy tummy feel a whole lot better!

Take a PICNIC CARD from your LUNCHBOX. Now go to 185.

Waiting outside was making Anne even more nervous than ever and so *she* offered to enter the lighthouse first. She immediately found herself at the bottom of a spiral stairway and she led the way up the crumbling steps. Eventually, they reached a small dusty room. 'It looks like this was the keeper's living-quarters,' Julian said, noticing a rusty old bed there. 'I wonder if it's where the treasure is hidden as well?' They didn't come across any gold or silver in the room, unfortunately, but they *did* find a coded message, chalked on the dusty floor!

*Use your **CODEBOOK CARD** to find out what the message said by decoding the instruction below. If you don't have a **CODEBOOK** in your **RUCKSACK**, go to 60 instead.*

+F
YPMNY

235

Julian immediately reached back to feel in his rucksack for his measuring tape but all he felt was a fluffy head. Of course, he had forgotten he was carrying Timmy there! His measuring tape was somewhere underneath Timmy and, since it would have been quite impossible to get to, he asked Anne to lend him hers. *Go to 206.*

Julian concentrated so hard on counting the paces that he didn't really look where he was putting his feet. At pace forty-three, he absent-mindedly stepped on a loose rock and toppled over! 'Oh no, I think my torch is broken!' he gasped as he heard the sound of tinkling glass coming from his rucksack. Fortunately, they counted out the rest of the paces without any further mishap and soon reached the path which the coastguard had described.

If you have it, remove the TORCH CARD from your RUCK-SACK. Now go to 2.

'Ooh, I don't like it in here!' Anne remarked as they all flashed their torches round the inside of the pill-box. 'Try and find that note as quickly as possible so that we can get out again.' Fortunately, it wasn't long before one of them did find the note, Julian spotting it by his feet. 'I don't know what you're going to be like when we explore the caves,' Dick teased Anne gently when they were outside again, beginning to follow the note's direction. 'They'll be much darker than that pill-box!' *Go to 200.*

Finding the youth hostel on their maps, they saw that it was only another half mile or so to the part of the coast opposite the lighthouse. As they were just about to leave the youth hostel, Timmy suddenly spotted a round leather case near the bottom of the flagpole. 'What's that you've found, Timmy?' George asked, taking it from him. 'Why, it's an old measuring tape! It must have been dropped by one of the hostellers in the days when the hostel was open.'

If you don't already have it, put the MEASURE CARD into your RUCKSACK. Now go to 42.

Timmy reached Jeremiah Boogle's cottage first, panting at the ramshackle door. 'What ye be wanting with ol' Jeremiah?' a man with a thick white beard asked when the children had knocked on this door. When Julian told him that they would like to borrow his rowing-boat, he said that it would cost them a pound. The children happily paid him the money and were soon rowing the little boat out to sea. They were about halfway to the tiny rocky island on which the lighthouse stood, when Anne noticed a coded message chalked near her feet!

Use your CODEBOOK CARD to find out what the message said by decoding the instruction below. If you don't have a CODEBOOK in your RUCKSACK, go to 171 instead.

Julian wanted them to take out their codebooks to work out the message on the knuckleduster but the others said they ought to use every second they had in looking for the treasure. He therefore slipped it into his pocket so he could work it out later. The children explored every inch of the small dusty room but there wasn't a single piece of treasure to be found. 'That dust has gone right down my throat,' complained George, spluttering. 'I'm going to have to drink some of my ginger beer to get rid of it!'

Take a PICNIC CARD from your LUNCHBOX. Now go to 62.

241

They were still trying to decide who should go first into the lighthouse when Anne suddenly screamed. They hadn't pulled their boat up high enough on to the rocks and it was just about to be washed away! Fortunately, they just managed to drag it up to safety before another wave came in. After that near disaster, entering the lighthouse didn't seem to matter so much and so Julian led the way into the dark interior. They were immediately met by a spiral staircase but they had only climbed a few of the steps when Julian thought he heard a slight movement just above them. 'Quick, get out a torch!' he exclaimed.

Use your TORCH CARD to find out who or what it is by placing exactly over the shape below – then follow the instruction. If you don't have a TORCH in your RUCKSACK, go to 128 instead.

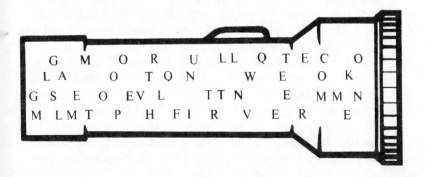

242

As Dick leaned down to try and reach into George's rucksack, however, he dropped the torch he was carrying. Fortunately, it just missed George's head but it continued falling until it disappeared into the darkness below. 'That's the end of my torch!' he remarked with a sigh. 'Even if we manage to find it again, it's sure to be in little pieces!' He told George that they would just have to forget about the coded message – trying to reach for her codebook could mean that it was *he* who fell next time!

If you have it, remove the TORCH CARD from your RUCK-SACK. Now go to 31.

243

While they were still trying to find a torch in their rucksacks, Timmy started sniffing at something on the ground. Then he picked it up in his teeth, carrying it over to George. 'Timmy, what's that you've found?' she asked, trying to work it out in the dark. 'Hey, it feels like a lamp! Quick, Julian, strike one of those matches you're carrying!' As soon as Julian's match had confirmed that it was indeed a lamp, he used the match to light it as well. 'Hurray, now we don't need waste our torches!' said Anne as they carried it with them. To celebrate their find, George passed round her ginger beer on the way.

Take a PICNIC CARD from your LUNCHBOX. Now got to 207.

Dick had only led them a very short way along the tunnel when he noticed a message at his feet. It was made up of lots of tiny pebbles and read: *BEWARE DANGEROUS HOLE 70 METRES FURTHER ON*. He turned round to tell the others about it, saying they had better take out one of their measuring tapes!

*Use your **MEASURE CARD** to measure the seventy metres from the pebbles – then follow the instruction there. If you don't have a **MEASURE** in your **RUCKSACK**, you'll have to guess which instruction to follow.*

Go to 144

Go to 207

Go to 97

Dick had just counted out the fifty-third pace from the message on the rock when George suddenly shouted something from behind. '*Now* who's making people lose their footing?' he asked, turning round crossly. 'You nearly made me jump out of my skin!' George went rather red. All she had wanted to do was show the others a water-skier down below! Dick was about to start counting again but suddenly forgot what number he was up to. They would all just have to go back to the message and start again! *Go to 103.*

246
'Listen a moment!' the sergeant suddenly said while the children were still looking for their maps. 'What's that faint gurgling sound? I know – it's the river!' He quickly led the way towards it, saying they didn't need their maps after all. 'The stone bridge crosses the river,' he explained as they went, 'so all we have to do is follow it!' When they reached the river they stopped for a short while to recover their breath before continuing. The run had made George so hot that she had to have a quick drink of her ginger beer as well!

Take a PICNIC CARD from your LUNCHBOX. Now go to 99.

The children were just about to take their maps from their rucksacks when George stopped them. 'There's no need to look up the way to the lighthouse,' she told them. 'I know the coastline to the left fairly well and there's certainly not a lighthouse in that direction. So it must be to the right!' The children therefore left their maps where they were, trusting George's judgment. *Go to 199.*

Obviously deciding it was safer if *he* led the way, Timmy went to the front along the path! The children hadn't been following him far when George pointed at a small lifeboat not far out to sea. 'The captain of that lifeboat is a friend of mine,' she said. 'Let's flash him a signal in Morse code and ask how much further round the lighthouse is. All we need is a torch!' At that, she immediately started to look for her torch in her rucksack.

Do you have a TORCH in your RUCKSACK? If so, use it to flash this Morse code signal by placing exactly over the shape below – then follow the instruction. If you don't have one, go to 101 instead.

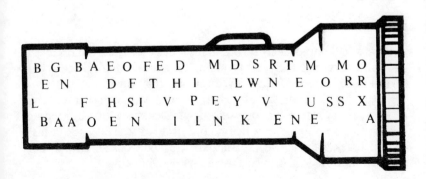

'I know what those bangs are!' Julian suddenly exclaimed. 'They're from an army shooting range. You often find them in deserted places like this!' As the bangs echoed round them again, the others felt sure that Julian was right. 'Just to be absolutely certain, though,' Dick suggested, 'let's see if there's one shown on our maps!' They all shrugged their rucksacks off their backs so they could take out their maps.

Use your MAP to find out which square the army shooting range is in – then follow the instruction. If you don't have one, you'll have to guess which instruction to follow.

If you think D3	go to 122
If you think D2	go to 201
If you think B3	go to 90

Dick had immediately turned to his rucksack to take out his map but George suddenly stopped him. 'Oh, no you don't, Dick!' she mocked him from behind. 'We all realise this is just your excuse to put off exploring the cave for a bit. We can leave looking it up on our maps until later, as you jolly well know!' Dick was so embarrassed at having been found out, that he put his map straight back in his rucksack again. However, as he did so, his codebook fell out, and he continued to lead the way forward without noticing it!

If you have it, remove the CODEBOOK CARD from your RUCKSACK. Now go to 284.

251

Julian arrived at Jeremiah Boogle's cottage first, knocking on the small wooden door. 'I'm sorry to disturb you,' Julian said politely when an old woman answered, 'but we wondered if your husband could lend us his rowing-boat?' The old woman told them that her husband wasn't in at present. 'He be gone to the ship's bell on the cliff-top,' she croaked. 'He go there once a week to give it a good polish. Loves that bell he do!' So they would know roughly how long they would have to wait until Jeremiah's return, the children decided to look up the ship's bell on their maps.

Use your MAP to find out which square the ship's bell is in – then follow the instruction. If you don't have a MAP in your RUCKSACK, you'll have to guess which instruction to follow.

If you think E4	go to 175
If you think E3	go to 213
If you think E2	go to 280

As Anne searched for her measuring tape, however, there was a sudden shower of rain which washed the message off the window! She desperately tried to remember what it had said but it had completely gone out of her mind. She couldn't remember whether it had said to walk *twenty metres* around the wall – or thirty or forty. Having a drink of ginger beer to console herself, she decided she would just have to forget about it, hoping it was nothing important!

Take a PICNIC CARD from your LUNCHBOX. Now go to 62.

'Is that any better, Anne?' Dick asked when, the first to find his torch, he had switched it on. Anne said that it was a lot better – she could now see a good ten steps in front! As she started to climb them again, she turned her head to ask how people managed to see their way up in the old days, when the lighthouse was in use. 'Well, they certainly wouldn't have had torches,' considered Julian. 'I suppose they must have carried either lamps or flares.' **Go to 12.**

The children were wondering how on earth Timmy was going to climb down the shaft but then Dick remembered having seen a length of rope in one of the lighthouse's rooms. Having rushed up the stairs to fetch it, he explained how they could make the rope into a sort of harness for Timmy and lower him down. As soon as this was done, they all quickly climbed into the shaft themselves. They had only descended about a dozen of the rungs, however, when Anne noticed a message on the shaft's rocky side. It read: *MEASURE EXACTLY 40 METRES STRAIGHT DOWN.*

Use your MEASURE CARD to measure these forty metres – then follow the instruction there. If you don't have one in your RUCKSACK, you'll have to guess which instruction to follow.

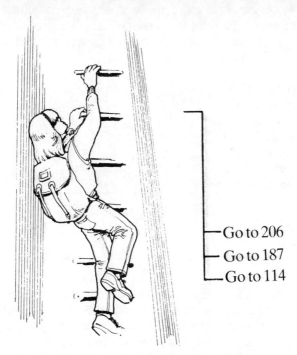

Go to 206
Go to 187
Go to 114

255

Dick found his torch first and immediately switched it on, pointing it at Julian and the object. 'Why, it's an old lamp!' Julian exclaimed. 'I wonder if it works? Hang on, I've got a box of matches somewhere!' As soon as he had found it, he struck a match and held it to the lamp's wick. It lit perfectly and was soon burning with a bright, steady glow. Julian suggested they take the lamp along the tunnel with them, using it instead of their torches. It would save their batteries! ***Go to 207.***

256
They all hurried in the direction of the stone bridge, finally spotting it ahead. They noticed several shadowy figures standing around. 'That's obviously the gang!' the sergeant whispered tensely as he made them all quickly hide behind some large boulders. 'We'll wait here until their plane arrives. I want to make sure we catch the pilot as well!' ***Go to 134.***

257
'Oh, *I'll* enter first!' George said impatiently and she immediately led the way through the lighthouse's door. As soon as she came to the spiral stairway that led to the top, however, she pushed Dick in front! 'I only said I'd *enter* first,' she told him, chuckling. 'You can go first now!' Rather reluctantly, Dick did so, leading the way up the crumbling steps. 'Hey, look, there's a message,' he said, suddenly noticing some chalked writing on one of them. 'I think we had better get out our measuring tapes. It says that we should beware forty metres further up!'

Use your MEASURE CARD to measure the forty metres from

the message – then follow the instruction there. If you don't have a MEASURE in your RUCKSACK, you'll have to guess which instruction to follow.

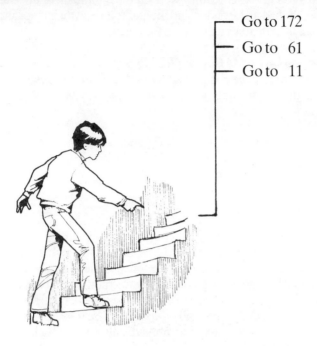

— Go to 172

— Go to   61

— Go to   11

258
The sergeant told Julian there wasn't time to decode the message on the sheet, however. 'There's not a moment to lose,' he said and he quickly led the way up the steps towards the top of the cliff. 'It's essential that we reach that stone bridge before the gang's plane does,' the sergeant added. 'We can come back and work out this message later!' *Go to 51.*

259
The children were still arguing over who was to go all the way across to the bird-watcher when they heard someone shout 'Fore' some distance over to their left. Then they saw a small white ball rise up

from behind a ridge. 'It must be a golf course behind there,' remarked Julian. Then he realised that they needn't ask the bird-watcher whether they were on the right track or not after all. All they had to do was look up the golf course on their maps and *that* would tell them exactly where they were!

Do you have a MAP in your RUCKSACK? If so, use it to find out which square the golf course is in – then follow the instruction. If you don't have one, you'll have to guess which instruction to follow.

If you think B3	go to 105
If you think A3	go to 288
If you think B2	go to 39

260

When Julian tried to decode the writing on the rock, however, he found that the symbols used were totally different to the ones in his codebook. It wasn't a total disappointment, though, because at the bottom of the writing a small arrow was scratched. Maybe that showed which direction Wailing Lighthouse was! So, remembering which way it pointed, he immediately hurried back to inform the others. *Go to 200.*

261

It was only a few seconds after George had flashed her Morse code signal to the lifeboat that they received a reply. 'It's saying that the lighthouse is about another three miles,' Julian slowly interpreted as the lifeboat flashed back at them. They continued on their way but hadn't gone much further when Anne stopped suddenly to pick something up from the grass. 'Look, someone's dropped their map!' she exclaimed.

If you don't already have it, put the MAP into your RUCK-SACK. Now go to 2.

Unlike the others, very little frightened Timmy and so *he* went into the cave first. 'Be careful you don't slip, everybody,' warned George as she followed close behind her dog. It was while she was watching her feet that Anne noticed a faded photograph on the cave's rocky floor. It was of some cliffs, and just out to sea was a shipwreck sticking out of the water. The children decided to see if the shipwreck was shown on their maps.

Use your MAP to find out which square the shipwreck is in– then follow the instruction. If you don't have a MAP in your RUCKSACK, you'll have to guess which instruction to follow.

If you think E3	go to 27
If you think E4	go to 76
If you think D4	go to 6

Julian just managed to reach the door of the youth hostel first. 'I'm afraid you can't book in until after 4 o'clock this afternoon,' said a man with a kindly, bearded face, who was sweeping the floor inside. He was obviously the warden. Julian told him that they merely wanted to enquire how much further it was to Wailing Lighthouse. 'Well, let me see,' the warden considered, scratching his beard.

'The quickest route is no more than half a mile. Just follow the little footpath 140 paces from our flagpole.'

Use your MEASURE CARD to measure the 140 paces from the flagpole – then follow the instruction there. If you don't have a MEASURE in your RUCKSACK, you'll have to guess which instruction to follow.

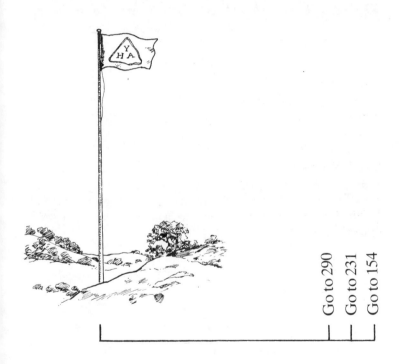

Go to 290

Go to 231

Go to 154

264

At last locating the lamp's wick, Julian took a box of matches from his rucksack and lit it. 'I've done it!' he exclaimed as the lamp suddenly flared up. All they had to do now was sit and wait. It would be getting dark soon and then the lamp would be visible for miles! While they were waiting, Dick suddenly spotted a group of men on the cliff-tops, walking hurriedly past a picnic site. He told the others to look up the picnic site on their maps, to see if it was on the way to the stone bridge. If it was, then these men were almost certainly the ones they had heard in the cave!

Use your MAP to find out which square the picnic site is in – then follow the instruction. If you don't have a MAP in your RUCKSACK, you'll have to guess which instruction to follow.

If you think C1	go to 50
If you think D1	go to 132
If you think C2	go to 98

265

Having found the stone tower on their maps, they saw that they were now almost halfway to the lighthouse. 'Now, everyone, remember which direction it is,' Julian told them before they started climbing down again. 'Don't forget we'll no longer be able to see it from the bottom!' *Go to 39.*

They were just about to switch on their torches, when they became aware of a horrible smell in the room. 'I know what this room is!' said Dick, holding his nose. 'That smell is oil and so this must be the oil-room! Let's just continue up the steps. I very much doubt whether the treasure's in here!' Even when they had left the room, however, the oil smell seemed to linger in their nostrils, giving them a horrible taste in their mouths as well. 'I think we'd better have some of my ginger beer to get rid of it,' said Anne.

Take a PICNIC CARD from your LUNCHBOX. Now go to 12.

Julian hurriedly told the sergeant about the gang in the cave and how they were looting all the treasure. 'It must have been them who locked that door you've just had to break down,' he said. 'They probably saw us when we were exploring the caves and realised we were interested in the treasure too. So they locked us in here to keep us out of the way!' The sergeant immediately escorted the children down to the bottom of the lighthouse and into the police motor-boat that was waiting outside. 'Right, let's just hope we can reach this stone bridge before the gang's plane does,' he said urgently as the boat raced through the water. 'Treasure-looting and locking people up are both serious offences!' *Go to 225.*

268

It was agreed that Julian's idea sounded best – just to keep following the coastline. That way, they were bound to reach the lighthouse eventually. Julian hadn't led them very far, however, when Anne suddenly thought of a flaw in his plan. 'What if we're following the coastline in the wrong direction, though?' she objected. Julian agreed it was a good point of Anne's and said they had better look up the lighthouse on their maps. Then they would know for certain which direction to go!

Do you have a MAP in your RUCKSACK? If so, use it to find out which square the lighthouse is in – then follow the instruction. (Remember to put the MAP back in your RUCKSACK afterwards.) If you don't have a MAP, you'll have to guess which instruction to follow.

If you think D1	go to 20
If you think E2	go to 247
If you think E1	go to 118

269

George was so excited as she opened her rucksack that she didn't notice a loose stone beneath her feet. 'Goodness, we just grabbed you in time!' Julian said with alarm as she nearly fell over the edge. Although they were able to save George, though, they didn't manage to save the coin she was holding. As she stumbled, it had dropped from her fingers! Nor was that the only thing to go over the cliff. Julian's torch had slipped out of his rucksack as he grabbed at George and now lay in tiny pieces way, way below!

If you have it, remove the TORCH CARD from your RUCK-SACK. Now go to 137.

270

'Oh, what a nuisance,' Julian tutted once they had opened their codebooks. 'This code is totally different to the one in our books!' They therefore decided that one of them would just have to go and ask the bird-watcher after all. This tricky task was given to George! To begin with the bird-watcher wouldn't help her but, after George apologised about Timmy, he slowly warmed. She eventually learnt that they *were* going the right direction for Wailing Lighthouse and went back to inform the others. She was in such a hurry, however, that she tripped on a small hole in the ground. Fortunately, she wasn't hurt – but she failed to notice that her measuring tape had slipped from her rucksack as she fell!

If you have it, remove the MEASURE CARD from your RUCKSACK. Now go to 39.

'Ugh – look at all that dust!' remarked George as she swung her torch beam across the hostel's filthy floor. 'I'm glad we're not going to spend a night in here!' Pointing her torch into one of the corners, she suddenly spotted Dick's ginger beer bottle. 'Here it is!' she exclaimed, handing it back to him. 'You're lucky it's not broken, Dick.' So that they didn't have any further mishaps in the hostel, they immediately continued on their way. *Go to 154.*

272

The children were still debating who should enter the lighthouse first when they heard an echoing 'Woof' from inside. Timmy had already gone in! Not half as anxious about it now, they walked through the door themselves, immediately coming to a stone stairway which spiralled upwards towards the top. They had climbed about a third of the way up the steps when they came to a small, very deep-set window. Peering through it, they could just see the top of a tall chimney in the distance. Dick suggested they look it up on their maps so they would know which direction they were facing.

Use your MAP to find out which square the chimney is in – then follow the instruction. If you don't have a MAP in your RUCKSACK, you'll have to guess which instruction to follow.

If you think B2	go to 112
If you think C2	go to 82
If you think C1	go to 12

Being the first to find her torch, George quickly switched it on and passed it forward to Julian. 'Perhaps I was just mistaken,' he said uncertainly as he took it from her and directed its beam above them. 'There doesn't *appear* to be anything there. Still, I think I'd better keep hold of your torch, George – just in case!' *Go to 12.*

Julian replied there was no time to wait, however. It would be evening in an hour or so and then they really would be in trouble if they hadn't found a way out. Anne agreed with him – she certainly did not fancy the idea of staying in that horrible lighthouse all night! So she decided to leave the coded message, hurriedly following the others down the shaft. Timmy found the descent the easiest – because Dick had had the clever idea of carrying him in his rucksack! *Go to 216.*

They now walked along the bay at the cliff bottom, and were surprised to find several very small cottages there. 'They must belong to fishermen,' said Julian, as they passed them on their way to the far end of the narrow bay. It was at this far end, where the waves were at their wildest, that the two caves were. *Go to 214.*

276

The children had still to open their maps when the sergeant suddenly spotted an old building in the distance. 'I won't be needing your maps after all!' he exclaimed. 'That's the old mill over there – which means the river must be there as well. The stone bridge crosses the river. So all we have to do is follow it!' Before they set off towards the mill, however, George quickly finished off her ginger beer so she could put the bottle into a rubbish bin that was there. It would make her lunchbox a lot easier to carry!

Take a PICNIC CARD from your LUNCHBOX. Now go to 99.

The children were still searching for their maps in their rucksacks when George gave a little cry. 'Hey, we don't need to look up our maps,' she exclaimed. 'I've just realised that I *know* the way to Whitedunes campsite!' She immediately led them round to the back of Kirrin Bay and then along a small path to an area of grassland. 'Here it is,' she said as they stood amongst a dozen or so tents. 'And, since I've been so clever, I think I deserve a drink from my bottle of ginger beer!'

Take a PICNIC CARD from your LUNCHBOX. Now go to 53.

The children were just about to start looking for their torches when they heard a loud scampering noise across the floor. 'It sounds like rats,' remarked Dick in alarm. 'Quick, let's get out of here!' The only one who wasn't in a hurry to leave was Timmy. He was keen to give the rats a good chase! George eventually persuaded him to come outside with them by promising him a large slice of her cherry cake. 'There – that's much better than chasing rats, isn't it?' she asked, as Timmy happily munched away in the sunshine!

Take a PICNIC CARD from your LUNCHBOX. Now go to 154.

Deciding she would much rather be at the front in the cave than at the back, *Anne* eventually volunteered to enter first. 'Now, make sure you all keep really close to me,' she told them nervously as she led the way through the gaping hole. To begin with there was enough light from the hole to see where they were going but as they ventured further and further in, it started to grow a lot darker. 'I think it's time to switch on our torches,' said Anne, and they all slipped off their rucksacks so they could take their torches out.

*Use your **TORCH CARD** to help light up the cave by placing exactly over the shape below – then follow the instruction. If you don't have a **TORCH** in your **RUCKSACK** go to 152 instead.*

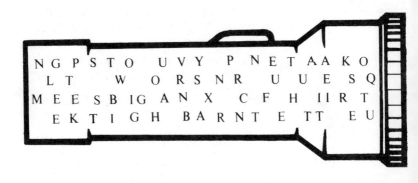

```
N G P S T O     U V Y     P   N E T   A A   K O
  L T       W     O R S N R       U   U E   S Q
M E E   S B  IG  A N   X     C   F   H    II R   T
   E K T  I  G H     B A R  N T   E    TT       E U
```

They were just about to dig through their rucksacks for their maps when Jeremiah Boogle appeared. He had a thick white beard and a pipe sticking out of the corner of his mouth. He was quite happy to lend them his rowing-boat, even refusing payment for it. 'Well, at least take a slice of cherry cake each!' insisted Julian, opening his lunchbox. The old couple joyfully accepted, looking as if they hadn't had the luxury of cake for years!

*Take a **PICNIC CARD** from your **LUNCHBOX**. Now go to 10.*

281

It was so windy on the lighthouse's balcony, however, that it was impossible to open their maps! 'Mine's blowing all over the place,' cried Anne as she struggled to hold on to it. 'We'd better put them back again before they get blown away or torn in half!' So this is exactly what they did, agreeing to look up the stack of stones when they had returned to Kirrin Cottage! *Go to 158.*

282

Thinking they would be stuck there all day otherwise, *Dick* eventually offered to enter the lighthouse first. The others followed him towards a stone stairway and then up the spiral steps until they came out at a small circular room. 'It looks like it was once the storeroom,' said Julian, as he looked around at all the old crates and boxes. While the others started to investigate these, Anne walked over to the small window to see how high up they were. She had just managed to push the stiff frame open when she suddenly noticed a message written in the dust on the glass. It read: *MEASURE OUT 40 METRES AROUND THE WALL*.

Use your MEASURE CARD to measure these forty metres – then follow the instruction there. If you don't have a MEASURE CARD in your RUCKSACK, you'll have to guess which instruction to follow.

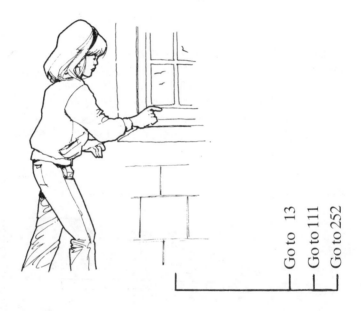

Go to 13
Go to 111
Go to 252

283

It looks as if this was the lighthouse's storeroom,' said Dick as their torches lit the place up. 'Look at all those boxes there!' The boxes would have made a good place to conceal the treasure and so they decided to give them a quick search. There wasn't any gold or silver in them, unfortunately – but one *did* contain a map, hidden under some old tins! They thought they might as well take it with them as a spare.

If you don't already have it, put the MAP into your RUCK-SACK. Now go to 12.

284

The Five ventured deeper and deeper into the cave, feeling their way along the damp slimy wall. 'There's certainly no sign of any treasure yet,' said Julian as they all peered through the darkness. 'Could it be buried under the ground somewhere or hidden in some cranny in this wall?' They all nearly jumped out of their skins as this question was suddenly answered by a strange voice from behind! 'It be neither,' it chuckled. The children quickly went for their torches so they could see to whom this scary voice belonged!

Use your TORCH to try and illuminate this person by placing exactly over the shape below – then follow the instruction. If you don't have a TORCH in your RUCKSACK, go to 91 instead.

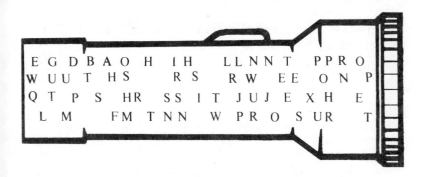

285

They were still trying to feel for their torches in their rucksacks when Anne suddenly touched something with her foot! 'Look, I've found an old oil-lamp,' she called to the others after she had bent down to investigate, 'and a box of matches as well!' Despite its age, the lamp lit perfectly and so they decided they might as well use it instead of one of their torches. They now set off along the tunnel – but without Dick's measuring tape. Unknown to him, it had fallen out while he had been feeling through his rucksack!

If you have one, remove the MEASURE CARD from your RUCKSACK. Now go to 207.

286

As soon as he had been handed a torch, Julian shone it where he had been pointing. 'Oh, you were right, Julian,' Anne exclaimed as the beam picked the cliff steps out. 'I can see them as clearly as anything now!' The police boat immediately came ashore and they all hurried towards the steps. They were about halfway up when Timmy picked something up in his mouth. 'What's that you've got, boy?' the sergeant asked as he took it from him. 'Well, well, well – it's a book of secret codes. I wouldn't mind betting this belongs to one of that gang!'

If you don't already have it, put the CODEBOOK CARD into your RUCKSACK. Now go to 217.

287

As Julian opened out his map, however, it was suddenly caught by a strong gust of wind. In trying to hold on to it, he was blown right up to the edge of the cliff. 'Oh Julian, watch out!' the others all cried together. Julian had to think fast and he threw himself to the ground just in time. He didn't stand up again until the gust was completely gone. 'It sounds like I've broken my torch,' he said glumly as he heard glass rattle in his rucksack. 'Still, I suppose it could have been much worse!'

If you have it, remove the TORCH CARD from your RUCK-SACK. Now go to 2.

The children were putting their maps away again when another 'Fore' was called and another golf ball went shooting up from behind the ridge. George was so intent on watching the ball's flight that she leant her head right back and made herself over-balance! 'George, what an idiot you are – everything's spilt out of your rucksack!' the others all laughed as they helped her repack it. Unfortunately, though, her codebook was half-hidden by the grass and they unknowingly set off again without it.

*If you have it, remove the **CODEBOOK CARD** from your **RUCKSACK**. Now go to 39.*

With the aid of a head start, because she was the youngest, *Anne* was the first to reach the youth hostel door. When the others arrived as well, they tried to open the door but found that it was locked. Although there was no one about, Dick thought of another way in which the youth hostel could help them in finding out how much further the lighthouse was. All they had to do was look it up on their maps!

*Use your **MAP** to find out which square the youth hostel is in – then follow the instruction. If you don't have a **MAP** in your **RUCKSACK**, you'll have to guess which instruction to follow.*

If you think D3	go to 42
If you think C2	go to 26
If you think D2	go to 238

290

Having counted the 140 paces from the youth hostel flagpole, The Five couldn't *see* any footpath! 'We'd better go back and ask the warden if he gave us the right number,' Dick suggested. To begin with, the warden couldn't understand it, insisting that 140 paces was definitely the correct distance. Then he suddenly realised! 'Of course – my stride is a lot bigger than yours!' he chuckled. Before they went looking for the footpath again, Julian offered the warden a large slice of his cherry cake for all his help.

Take a PICNIC CARD from your LUNCHBOX. Now go to 154.

291

They were just about to start measuring the forty metres round the wall, when Dick realised there was a problem. 'Which *way* do we measure?' he asked. 'The message doesn't say whether it's clockwise or anti-clockwise!' Julian scratched his head for a moment, agreeing that this was a good point. 'Well, we'll just have to measure both ways,' he eventually replied. 'First we'll try clockwise and, if that doesn't lead to anything, we'll do anti-clockwise.' *Go to 13.*

292

The Five had just got to pace forty when they all froze in their tracks. There was a horrible wailing sound from the lighthouse as a sudden gust of wind blew up! 'Are you sure we ought to row over there?' Anne asked anxiously but Julian said that they shouldn't let a bit of wind bother them. 'Come on – let's continue with these paces!' he told them all encouragingly. *Go to 44.*

'It says that there is something that could well be very useful ten rungs down!' Anne told the others excitedly when she had decoded the message on the iron ring. 'Perhaps it's a spare key to the door!' So Julian hurriedly climbed down to the tenth rung but all he found there was an old map of the area, wedged between the rung and the wall. Nevertheless, he popped it into his rucksack in case they lost one of theirs! The others now came into the shaft after him, Dick having had the clever idea of carrying Timmy down in his rucksack!

If you don't already have it, put the MAP into your RUCK-SACK. Now go to 216.

While the others were still looking for their torches, however, Julian suddenly remembered he was carrying a box of matches on him. So he struck one near the object. 'Why, it's an old lamp!' he exclaimed, and he quickly used the match to light it. He told the others that they could stop searching for their torches now – but Dick continued to rummage through his rucksack, saying that they would need one anyway for going along the tunnel. 'Idiot!' the others all laughed at him. 'We can use this lamp now, can't we?' *Go to 207.*

They were still waiting for someone to pluck up the courage to lead the way into the cave when Timmy started sniffing at an old oil drum washed up on to the beach. 'Timmy, leave that nasty thing alone!' George commanded, walking over so she could drag him away from it. When she reached the drum, however, she noticed that there was a coded message scratched across its surface. 'Well spotted, Timmy!' she apologised, as they all hurriedly looked for their codebooks.

Use your CODEBOOK CARD to find out what the message said by decoding the instruction below. If you don't have a CODEBOOK in your RUCKSACK, go to 169 instead.

George had only led them a few steps along the dark tunnel when she stopped. 'I think we'd better get out one of our torches,' she said. Just at that moment, Julian slipped on something on the tunnel floor! 'It feels like a candle,' he said as he picked himself up again. 'I've got a box of matches with me. I'll just strike one and see!' It *was* a candle and so Julian quickly used the match to light it. 'Hey, there's some sort of coded message scratched along it as well,' he exclaimed as it started to burn. 'Quick, someone, pass me a codebook!'

Use your CODEBOOK CARD to find out what the message on the candle said by decoding the instruction below. If you don't have a CODEBOOK in your RUCKSACK, go to 49 instead.

'It says that this coin was part of the treasure taken from the *White Rose* wreckage,' Dick announced excitedly, when he was the first to decode the message on the coin. Julian, after thinking about this for a moment, said that the code must have been scratched on it by one of those evil men responsible for the wrecking. 'It's probably a sort of secret identification mark they put on some of the coins,' he suggested. *Go to 137.*

Before The Five had started their measuring, however, the man from the campsite appeared again. 'I just remembered,' he said, holding a large jerrycan, 'I needed to come over to the tap myself to fill up with water. Anyway, now that I'm here I might as well *show* you the footpath you want.' The children were very grateful for his help, Anne offering him a slice of her cherry cake to show this gratitude. 'Mm, it tastes delicious,' he said as he set them on their way.

Take a PICNIC CARD from your LUNCHBOX. Now go to 53.

The others all said they'd feel happier if Julian led the way himself. They hadn't gone far along the tricky path, however, when he suddenly brought them all to a halt. 'Be careful,' he warned, 'there's quite a deep hole just in front!' As he was stepping round the hole, he thought he saw something glimmer at the bottom. He knelt right down to the hole but he still couldn't make out what it was. 'I know!' Anne said, suddenly having an idea. 'We can use one of our torches!'

Do you have a TORCH in your RUCKSACK? If so, use it to try and find out what the object in the hole is by placing exactly over the shape below – then follow the instruction. If you don't have a TORCH CARD, go to 71 instead.

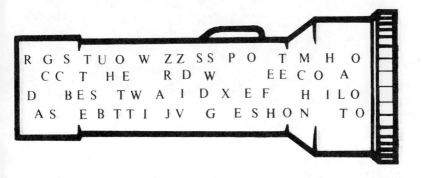

```
R G S  T U O  W  Z Z  S S  P O    T M  H  O
   C C  T  H E       R  D W          E E  C O  A
D     B E S   T W  A  I  D X  E F      H    I L O
   A S    E B T T I   J V    G   E  S H O N       T O
```

The undersea tunnel went on and on but then they suddenly had to come to a stop. There was a huge pile of boulders in front of them, impossible to pass! They were just about to collapse to the ground in despair when they heard voices from the other side of the boulders. 'I reckons that's all the treasure found now, then, lads,' one of them said. 'Let's shift it up to the stone bridge ready for the plane to collect us tonight. We'll be in France tomorrow and as rich as can be!' The children all looked at each other in amazement, wondering what to make of this. It was Julian who suddenly came up with an explanation! *Go to 113.*

301

The sergeant told the children not to bother about their torches, though, ordering his pilot to switch on the police boat's searchlight instead. 'There – that's a lot better than a torch, isn't it?' he chuckled as the bright beam moved along the cliffs. It soon reached the spot to which Julian had been pointing and proved he was right. The cliff steps *were* there! The boat therefore quickly came ashore and they all hurried towards them. *Go to 217.*

302

Although the glass door was a bit stiff, it finally gave and they walked out into the open air. 'Gosh, isn't it windy,' cried Dick, 'and look what a marvellous view you get! I wonder what that tall stack of stones is in the distance?' They decided to look it up on their maps to settle their curiosity.

Use your MAP to find out which square the tall stack of stones is in – then follow the instruction. If you don't have a MAP in your RUCKSACK, you'll have to guess which instruction to follow.

If you think A2	go to 47
If you think B2	go to 281
If you think A3	go to 158

'Look, they must be the caves!' Dick said, pointing to two large holes in the cliffs a short way to their left. 'Can you see? – right at the end of that narrow bay there. I wonder how we get down to it?' His answer was given by an old signpost which George spotted a little further along. It read: *CLIFF STEPS DOWN TO WAILING BAY – 90 METRES*. They immediately looked for their measuring tapes!

Use your MEASURE CARD to measure the ninety metres from the signpost – then follow the instruction there. If you don't have a MEASURE in your RUCKSACK, you'll have to guess which instruction to follow.

Go to 7

Go to 186

Go to 58

The children immediately asked Ebenezer how they could get to the lighthouse. He informed them that they could borrow a rowing-boat from Jeremiah Boogle, who lived in the nearest of the fishermen's cottages on the bay. After thanking Ebenezer, The Five hurried towards Jeremiah Boogle's!

Throw THE FAMOUS FIVE DICE to decide who is to reach Jeremiah Boogle's cottage first.

JULIAN thrown	go to 251
DICK thrown	go to 77
GEORGE thrown	go to 170
ANNE thrown	go to 59
TIMMY thrown	go to 239
MYSTERY thrown	go to 92

305

'I don't mind being the one to go,' Dick volunteered cheerfully and, without further ado, he ran across towards the bird-watcher. When he reached him, however, he found the bird-watcher wasn't half as helpful as he had expected. 'Wailing Lighthouse – why do you want to go there?' he demanded grumpily. 'I'd only tell the way to sensible people who were interested in it for its history – not to a kid like you who probably wants to mess about near it!' ***Go to 104.***

FAMOUS FIVE SERIES

FIVE ON A TREASURE ISLAND
FIVE GO ADVENTURING AGAIN
FIVE RUN AWAY TOGETHER
FIVE GO TO SMUGGLER'S TOP
FIVE GO OFF IN A CARAVAN
FIVE ON KIRRIN ISLAND AGAIN
FIVE GO OFF TO CAMP
FIVE GET INTO TROUBLE
FIVE FALL INTO ADVENTURE
FIVE GO ON A HIKE TOGETHER
FIVE HAVE A WONDERFUL TIME
FIVE GO DOWN TO THE SEA
FIVE GO TO MYSTERY MOOR
FIVE HAVE PLENTY OF FUN
FIVE ON A SECRET TRAIL
FIVE GO TO BILLYCOCK HILL
FIVE GET INTO A FIX
FIVE ON FINNISTON FARM
FIVE GO TO DEMON'S ROCKS
FIVE HAVE A MYSTERY TO SOLVE
FIVE ARE TOGETHER AGAIN

THE ENID BLYTON TRUST
FOR CHILDREN

We hope you have enjoyed the adventures of the children in this book. Please think for a moment about those children who are too ill to do the exciting things you and your friends do.

Help them by sending a donation, large or small, to the ENID BLYTON TRUST FOR CHILDREN. The Trust will use all your gifts to help children who are sick or handicapped and need to be made happy and comfortable.

Please send your postal orders or cheques to:

The Enid Blyton Trust For Children,
International House,
1 St Katherine's Way,
London E1 9UN

Thank you very much for your help.